The Ocean and the Wave

A Story of Spiritual Awakening

Roger Calverley

LOTUS PRESS

P O Box 325
Twin Lakes, WI 53181 USA

First Edition 2019

ISBN: 978-1-6086-9237-8

Library of Congress Number: 2019954683

Published by:

LOTUS PRESS

Lotus Press

P.O. Box 325
Twin Lakes, WI 53181 USA
800-824-6396 (toll free order phone)
262-889-8561 (office phone)
262-889-2461 (office fax)
www.lotuspress.com (website)
lotuspress@lotuspress.com

Printed In USA

Table of Contents

1

A Story of Spiritual Awakening

Have you ever entered a realm of experience within your own being where thoughts fade away, and you are left wide-eyed and filled with wonder? Have you ever found yourself gazing with rapt attention at nothing at all, fully conscious of everything around you, but effortlessly and completely at rest in a continuum of stillness?

Has your heart ever melted with love or gratitude as a smile burst out on your countenance, and you could only beam your joy in all directions? Have you ever known a state of contentment where words and thoughts could add nothing whatsoever to your feeling of fullness?

These and similar experiences make it clear that you have touched and spent precious moments in the deep recesses of your own being. These glimpses testify, beyond a shadow of doubt, that you have access to the domain of your infinite potential.

When you ponder the implication of such experiences, it is impossible to deny that you ARE already, in the core of your being, complete and perfect. You have what you seek. Your very essence is a condition of boundless fulfilment.

This experience of infinite consciousness, which we can all discover when we turn inward, is not merely a temporary modification of the mind or body. It is much more than that. It is the bliss of our fundamental nature.

If, even once in a lifetime, you have had such an experience it means that you have received a direct invitation from Source to come home, not some time in the future, but NOW, and not elsewhere, but HERE.

Why waste time trying to assemble or fabricate the bliss that is already present, perfect and complete in the very heart of existence? Why struggle and strive to acquire the symbols of the "good life" when we already have and are what we have been missing? Look within and ask: "What truly exists when everything falls silent?"

In the spacious sky of your mind, in the openness of your quiet awareness, thinking activity will naturally quiet down. The power of your inner stillness will come to the fore and offer you an experience of who and what you really are in the depth of your being and in the fullness of your potential. Over time, in the deepening of this experience, the following becomes very clear:

> *The path to liberation is as long or as short as the distance from the head to the heart, and as slow or as complicated as our thinking activity makes it. It is a journey in which no one goes anywhere, and no one is either lost or liberated, for when the one who dreams all of this wakes up, this dreaming protagonist is seen to be a fantasy. Dreams end, clarity dawns, awakening shines. It's that simple.*

Although in the pages which follow you will read sentences that refer to seekers and seeking, this kind of language is just a concession to the way things appear for a conventionally conditioned mind. Waves appear, but only the ocean exists.

Seeking, striving and attaining are all stories that the thinking mind creates about "me" and "my" in the context of its acquired mental conditionings, and only for the duration of the dream. Our cherished narratives, beliefs and projects, including spiritual projects, come to the end of their relevance when the ocean is recognized in all its waves.

Only the thinnest of veils prevents the thinking mind from seeing and knowing the fullness of the awakened heart and the spaciousness of consciousness liberated from belief in its contents.

Once mind-spun dreaming is seen for what it is, the ocean of infinite consciousness will begin to dissolve the constructs and fabrications which keep attention hypnotically bound to its own fantasies. Appearances continue, but in the silent core of the spiritual heart, belief-systems, journeys, and seeking-activity subside into the pristine existence of oneness with Source.

Will the dreaming mind continue to live on the ocean's restless surface where the waves are choppy and the joys fleeting? Or will it dive within and discover the blissful depths?

In the pages that follow, a story unfolds of one such journey inward to Source. It is an invitation to dive within and discover the unimaginable treasure that lies in the core of your very own being.

2

Foreword

Most of us love the ocean, the sound of its waves crashing against the shore, the smell of its salty waters, and its majestic vastness stretching beyond our line of sight.

But in and through all of its varied aspects, the ocean is an eternal wellspring of mystery and meaning. Some contemplatives have plumbed the depth of the ocean's song and expressed its ancient wisdom in words. I was fortunate enough to meet such a one and receive direct transmission of his timeless wisdom, which was the presence and power of the ocean of consciousness itself.

This early introduction to the wisdom of the ocean and the wave happened when I lived in a small cinder block hermitage overlooking the Gulf of Siam at Wat Kao Takiap just south of Hua Hin, Thailand.

In those peaceful days and weeks, I spent many hours in meditation, kept a journal, and soaked in the rhythmic cadence of the waves. All day and all night the waves washed against the base of the cliff below my abode, sending the fresh smell of salt spray up to the flat, paved area where I lived.

A quarter century later, back home in Canada, I came across the notes I had made of that time by the seaside, fresh with the smell of the salt spray, and vibrant with inspiration. I dusted off these old notebooks, opened them up and began to read. A world of insights and experiences came flooding back.

There, on those yellowing pages, penned almost three decades earlier in blue-black fountain-pen ink was a record of my first experience of the liberated state.

It all comes back to me now, the long meditations by the sea, the kind counsel of a wise and compassionate spiritual friend, the conversations, the insights, the vast starry sky above, the tropical moon ablaze in the night with borrowed light from the sun, and always the sound of the ocean marking time with the rhythmic cadence of its waves.

In those weeks of contemplative stillness overlooking the Gulf of Siam, I had been given the key to spiritual freedom, and had experienced its radiance in the spaciousness of an awakening mind and heart. There it was, clearly revealed in my notes and poems. Then, somehow, because of old tendencies, fixed commitments and a restless desire to travel and keep busy, I misplaced this manuscript and let its precious content slip from my awareness. Years of travel, teaching, reading and meditation intervened, with occasional glimpses of the state itself. But direct access and full, conscious possession of what had been experienced in those days had seemingly been lost.

Yet now, it all comes back so clearly and powerfully! And it can be stated in just a few words:

> *The liberated state is nothing more and nothing less than life, here and now, just AS IT IS, minus mind's illusory thoughts. However unrecognized or overlooked the true condition may appear to be, it is the only constant through all the varied waves of experience we fabricate and forget.*
>
> *The truth of our being is not elsewhere. Nor does it require that we strive and seek. Pure presence, radiantly aware, is alone true. Knowing this is wisdom; living it fully is love.*

What follows is the story of how the ocean's wisdom revealed itself in my life, in a context of spiritual seeking and meditative aspiration. It not only recounts my meetings with a wise teacher, the insights and experiences he shared, and our journeys of spiritual discovery together by the Gulf of Siam, it also attempts to re-awaken the magic, the beauty, the sweetness and the music of those weeks and months by the ocean-side, in a very different time and place. As I read and recall those words from the past, the now that was then rejoins the now that is here, and the song of the ocean invades my awareness once again.

3

My Story

My spiritual life falls into two halves. The first, lasting over a quarter century, was taken up by devotional meditation in a gradual path of love, devotion and surrender under an Indian guru. The second half, initiated by Lama Atal in Thailand, was a more sudden awakening to non-dual wisdom, insight into emptiness, and direct experience of the liberated state which transcends the thinking mind and all its categories.

As a child, I was drawn to a real but invisible, living "presence" which I could feel and almost glimpse, at times, in the sky, the forest trees and the waters of the St. Lawrence River which flowed not far from where I lived. Prior to my school years, I had memories of the angelic realms. Sometimes my sister and I would talk and recollect a "time before" this life in which we were appearing as physical bodies. For as long as I can remember, I was eager to get through my formal schooling quickly so that I would be free to pursue a calling to the contemplative life.

Within a year of graduating from university, I discovered that religious orders like the Jesuits or Dominicans could not offer what I was looking for, so I began to study and practice meditation with a guru from India, a Bengali who had been a student of the famous Sri Aurobindo.

After joining this guru's meditation group, there was an opening of the spiritual heart, and from this a flow of creative and mystical experiences revealing wide ranges of consciousness and glimpses of the inner worlds.

All of this helped to re-balance the intellectualism that had crept in while I was doing a double major four-year degree at the University of Toronto.

When the opportunity arose, I travelled to India, twice, and spent time at the ashrams of Sri Aurobindo and Sri Ramana Maharshi, luminaries who have inspired and guided my spiritual seeking over the years.

I became familiar with Theravada Buddhism while living in Thailand for five years in the 1990's, but felt more attracted to Tibetan Buddhism which I studied under the direction of Lama Lhanang Rinpoche in Canada. The deep wisdom of this tradition and the fact that it was actively practiced with great sincerity impressed me.

During my stay in Thailand, an opportunity arose to practice meditation in a secluded corner of a Thai monastery overlooking the Gulf of Siam. It was during this period of my life that I awakened to the wisdom of "The Ocean and the Wave". This, in turn, became the foundation for a fuller spiritual realization a number of years later.

Many factors came together to make my weeks of meditation, study and dialogue with Lama Atal in Thailand a powerfully transformative experience. It was not only his presence as a wise spiritual friend, or the precious teachings he shared, or our meditations, it was also the immediate presence of the ocean, singing its eternal song just below my hermitage over-looking the waters of the Gulf of Siam. Taken together, these elements made the experience something beautiful and memorable.

In the years which followed, there were many opportunities for travel and adventure. As I look back at the time spent in Peru, immersed in the Andean spiritual tradition, the meditation teachings I was invited to give in Canada, the USA, Australia, New Zealand and Southeast Asia, the discoveries with crystals and healing at a distance, I see the intervening years as a time of busyness.

The essence of the spiritual journey, however, has been one of letting go of distracting thinking-activity, and opening up to the reality which reveals itself in the core of the spiritual heart. Experiences arise and pass, natural wisdom steadily deepens. Insights points to what is true, but demonstrate also that ultimate Truth can never be grasped by the mind or adequately expressed in words.

The generation of teachers from India and Tibet who came west in the late 20th century has mostly passed away. From their long and deep practice, these adepts attained profound depths of realization, which seem mostly missing in meditators in the west, where distractions abound and family and career seem to take up the lion's share of available time.

Traditionally, teachers would spend many years drilling their students in preliminary practices for the sake of purification, self-discipline and transformation, modifying existing states of mind, improving the personality and developing other qualifications that presumably would lead to enlightenment. I practiced this way for years. It is called the 'gradual path', and it makes sense only when insight into the emptiness of self has not arisen.

The direct path is more radical. It is founded on the fact that the essence of our being is already perfect, primordially liberated and enlightened,requiring no transformation or improvement. This pristine continuum of Truth-consciousness is always present, behind our thinking activity. It is the indwelling essence of our being.

Once recognized, this pristine continuum of awareness stands self-revealed as the real refuge and the ultimate practice. In other words, the "goal" becomes the "path" and non-striving becomes the "technique". The point is not to develop a whole new set of mental conditionings, but rather to relax into to the perfection that is already present.

From the perspective of a beginner who feels a heartfelt call to self-realization, the path generally takes the mind through provisional teachings and contrived meditations to a more mature stage of non-striving and infused contemplation. From the perspective of what is true and ultimately real, talk of seekers and seeking, striving and attaining, paths and goals are all based on a fundamental misunderstanding of the truth of emptiness.

Stories such as this one can be provisionally useful if the dream character being imagined and sustained by the egoic mind can glimpse what waking up from the dream altogether really means. Located as we are in the human condition, it is in and through stories that we come to understand the nature of our experience. This is the story of one wave that awoke to its identity with the ocean of existence.

4

The Wave IS The Ocean

My first meditation teacher, a guru from India, asked me to start a meditation center in Thailand. I had been with him almost twenty-five years, and in that time I had met many practitioners who, after years of faithful practice, had not accomplished any definitive realization. They all continued to experience various forms of suffering, however attenuated.

At one point, I was brought face-to-face with the question of why these people, and seekers generally, were not able to achieve freedom through their practice.

The answer lay in the way they conceived their "enlightenment project", thinking of meditation as a solution to all manner of dissatisfactions with their experiences in life. As spiritual seekers, they were looking for relief from life's difficulties. Their teachers gave out meditation techniques to practice, readings to study, and occasional personal advice. The aspirant would talk with the teacher occasionally and receive ongoing counsel to address perceived issues as they arose. Good meditative experiences would be considered a sign of "progress". Periods of dryness were understood to be the necessary price for the good times. And so it would go.

This would go on for years in a kind of holding pattern where not much would change. The subject would still be seeking liberation or realization, and the teacher would be supporting the quest as the individual would attempt to deal with the various "issues" that would keep coming up.

The issues in play would take the form of questions such as: "Are my agitated thoughts and my troubled emotions diminishing? Are my "breakthrough" moments lasting longer and becoming more continuous? Are my troubles fading? Are my doubts and confusion clearing?"

The teacher would attempt to resolve and ameliorate these and similar concerns which the student would raise. This could happen in individual consultations or in a group setting. Either way, the process would be the same. The core idea was that if the "seeker" could "find" some "solutions", then "progress" would result. If issues such as those mentioned above could be resolved and the practitioner's concerns laid to rest, then attainment was closer. The meditator would, as a result of this process, presumably become a shining example of the success of the Dharma teachings. This would be considered "proof of concept." It would conclusively demonstrate that, by long and arduous application of advice and by consistent practice, the method would bring success.

I never met even one practitioner who had full success using this model. So I had to ask myself what was wrong. Was this kind of spiritual methodology really dispelling the ills of all these seekers? And what would a good result look like anyway? What form does a "liberated me" take?

The measuring stick used by teachers and students alike seemed to be their sense of well-being. In other words, if the individual felt better, had longer periods of inner stillness, fewer emotional problems, more success and less grief, that would be proof that the system had generated a "new, improved me".

This would indicate that these methods really worked. In all cases, this sustained self-improvement project, carried on to the point of complete release, was all about "me".

But the problem was and is that this approach has never, ever worked! I tried to understand why, and eventually found a key that shed light on the conundrum. My experience of the ocean and the wave overlooking the Gulf of Siam proved to be just such a key. The relationship of the ocean to the wave, rightly understood, resolves the subject/object dilemma which lies at the heart of the problem in this seeking-and-striving paradigm.

Simply put, there is no problem to begin with, because the wave IS the ocean, and the ocean is without problems of any kind.

Apart from thoughts and feelings about anything whatsoever, one never finds a "me" who has a "problem". The "me" that owns the difficulties simply does not exist and can never be identified. To summarize it all very succinctly, there is no wave that is not the ocean and no problem that can ever arise to an ocean.

Difficulties and issues are dependent on the one who "owns" the difficulties. But deep meditation reveals that, after dropping conceptual designations, and thought-narratives based on them, the imagined owner of the problems is actually a condition of pure being free of any liabilities or defects whatsoever.

There is no owner of the problem, only a story about self and its difficulties. There is no actual wave on the objective side, only the ocean appearing as impermanent waves, and these waves creating stories about supposed problems.

Thus there is no need for fictional selves to make efforts to solve fictional issues, just as there is no need for the ocean to strive to create better waves. There is no need to struggle for self- improvement or dedicate time and energy to an arduous and extended "enlightenment project."

"Improved waves" do not eventually get to be liberated waves. They are already and always only the ocean - which is, by its intrinsic nature, beyond both suffering and release.

Minus the concept of a fictional self, there is no one to own any issue, no one to struggle with any difficulty. Without the underpinning of an imagined "I" (the wave) and its stories about "me" (an activity we can call "waving", or "selfing"), all difficulties are clearly seen to be contrived and fictional. They are fantasies, nothing more.

Every wave is only the ocean, and the ocean is a continuous condition of pure being infinitely released from fictional dilemmas. Seeing this, wrong views rooted in beliefs about an imaginary self suddenly cease to have any meaning. Mental afflictions based on the idea that one could somehow be a wave rather than the ocean simply cease to be.

Once this is clearly recognized, "selfing" activity ends, "spiritual selfing" included. The endless cycles of seeking, striving, attaining and repeating no longer have any validity, and so they too fade and disappear.

A basic misunderstanding lies at the heart of efforts to improve the wave rather than to recognize that every wave is always and only the infinite ocean of peace, bliss and completeness. When recognized, this insight changes everything.

As currently taught, the various forms of Dharma seem to provisionally accept the validity of the separate "self", and teach that this self is an interdependent part of the whole. The teaching insists that the wave is 'part of the ocean' and therefore 'whole', or 'good'.

However, the validity of the notional self is not fundamentally challenged. On the basis of this misunderstanding, from this presumably valid starting point, a "seeker" then undertakes an "enlightenment-project" to transform a "distressed self" into a "problem-free self". The end result of such an 'enlightenment- project' would be a liberated wave, free of its egoic issues.

But consider: The wave already IS the ocean. There is no wave that is not already the ocean.

To be even more clear with regard to this critical point: *there is no wave.* A "wave" is only a conceptual label imposed by a thinking mind on the ocean. A wave is nothing more than a verbal designation. From these labels, it is possible to cook up many stories about defective waves and their suffering and striving and attaining, but the fact remains: there are no real waves.

There can never be a solution to a story that is a fiction. And therein lies the difficulty with Dharma teachings that try to create improved waves. Spiritual selfing does not liberate. Doing a lot of it does not change this stark fact. But insight into the actuality that every wave is always and only the ocean can and does change everything.

So the real starting point that could possibly resolve the conundrum at the root of spiritual seeking is the realization that no separate wave and separate self have ever existed. There is no wave that is not the ocean. And no ocean has ever had problems. Seeking and striving based on failure to recognize this point leads nowhere.

Making an imagined wave perfect is the proposed project. But this never, ever works because the ocean is already perfect. In fact, only the ocean exists, and the label "perfection" is superfluous. Study, practice and consultation with a teacher will not accomplish the impossible task of creating a "liberated" wave. How could the wave be liberated from its essential and pre-existing status as the ocean of existence-consciousness-bliss?

The only solution is to get beyond the notion that the wave is anything other than the ocean, and this comes by direct experience of the ocean in its immanence and fullness. This was the decisive factor in my time spent by the Gulf of Siam talking and meditating with Lama Atal.

By experiencing itself beyond all notions, all striving, all doing and all conceptual designations, the imaginary wave can come to know its non-existence in any meaningful way apart from the fact that it is identical to its very ground of being, the ocean of infinite consciousness, boundless love-wisdom inseparable.

Simply put, it is by letting go of what is not, and opening up to what IS that the ocean is realized as the only reality. By becoming still, the mind recognizes what IS and lets go of notions based on conceptual designations and stories sustainable only by more thinking-activity.

Bring the movements of the mind to stillness, and its waves invariably subside into their oceanic reality. But be very clear about one point: more and better "waving activity" will never liberate a fictional wave.

The key to this insight is to slow the mind down until the reality is clearly seen and thoroughly understood. Any form of non-doing which gears the mind down to a state of complete stillness will bring about this result.

At some point, on the basis of this letting go (of mental noise), along with opening up to what we recognize as the natural state, free of mental agitation, the subconscious mind will cease to generate the mistaken "me" belief.

This "me" idea was never anything other than a notion that waves could somehow be something other than the ocean. As long as the "selfing" activity of the wave is sustained, a story about being a wave seems credible. The fact that virtually all spiritual seekers do it and most teachers allow it does not help. However, once stillness generates real insight, the fictions fall apart.

There is no "wave" to become liberated. There is only the ocean of consciousness which has no need to become anything because it is already and eternally the ultimate state of pure Being. Seeing and understanding this clearly, one is freed from the "enlightenment project". There is no need for struggle, striving or attainment. There is no possibility of "liberation" or "enlightenment" once there is direct insight into what is real and what is not.

When wrong ideas about waves being separate from the ocean dissolve, the natural state, free of illusion, is all that remains. There is no one to claim it. It is as it is and cannot be otherwise, stories and fantasies notwithstanding. Apart from fictional notions about waves and "waving", that's the way it has always been, and no doubt will continue.

Thirty years have passed since Lama Atal first pointed my mind toward the wisdom of the Ocean and the Wave. Could it really have taken that long for his wise words and guided meditations to dissolve the mistaken ideas that fuelled my spiritual striving? How could I have set aside my notes and my recollections of his words and company for so many years and failed to understand how precious those insights and meditations really were?

Perhaps, as I recall and re-tell the story of our meeting and of our shared time together by the Gulf of Siam, an answer to this disturbing question will become clear.

5

Getting To The Ocean

When I was young, I thought that being a saint would be the formula for a life well lived. As a Catholic, I was taught that all humans are deeply compromised by sin. It seemed to me as a child that the best way to become a saint would be to discover a vocation as a priest and in this way avoid sin altogether, if at all possible. God approving, I could then hope for a good and reasonably happy life. It was a Catholic way of thinking.

My perspective on life didn't factor in any call to bliss so much as acceptance of the inevitability of suffering, with some good hope that it could be redemptive. The strength to endure, and the common sense to not mess things up counted for a lot in the view I inherited from church and family.

Shortly after I began studies to become a Jesuit, my mind widened into a new perspective. After reading a book called "Christian Yoga", I came to the conviction that liberation and enlightenment were not only possible, they were really what life was all about. I had to admit that I was not actually inspired by the prospect of a life spent marrying, burying and counselling people who took little interest in the things of God.

In my first few months of studying to be a priest, I began doing hatha yoga on a daily basis, undertook a vegetarian diet and made sincere efforts to meditate. Needless to say, at this point my lifestyle no longer conformed to what was expected of a typical Jesuit novice. One year or so into the novitiate, the novice master challenged my right to use my free time for spiritual practices that were not part of his program.

So I left the Jesuits and began a new phase of life with perfect freedom to explore spirituality in all its varied forms.

Toronto in the mid to late 1970's was an amazing place to be a young and aspiring spiritual seeker. Yoga studios and meditation groups were popping up everywhere. I was introduced to a guru from India who happened to live in New York and began to meditate daily. I also attended meetings at his local Toronto group and put in quite a few hours of service.

After years of spiritual striving, with unvarying meditation practice of one or two hours a day, my guru sent me to Thailand to open a meditation center in his name. That was where my non-dual awakening really began. There I felt totally free to follow my heart and my love of adventure.

6

Days of Great Peace

I had first visited Hua Hin in southern Thailand with my guru and a group of his students at Christmas time in 1988, and while there we befriended the abbot of a Buddhist monastery or Wat which was about two miles south of the town on a large hill overlooking the Gulf of Siam.

Since this abbot spoke English, he was my best contact, when I returned to Thailand, at the guru's request, to start a meditation center. The abbot welcomed me back to Wat Kao Takiap to meditate, orient, and plan the project. He was kind enough to let me use a small house on a cliff over-looking the Gulf of Siam where I could meditate and discern a way forward. The challenge was considerable since I was in a strange country and did not speak the language.

A stone's throw away from my new home was a cave where two monks spent their time meditating. One of the monks would see bright lights above him while sitting for practice, or while trying to sleep, and the other monk liked to practice a form of walking meditation which was widely popular in Thailand at that time.

Both of them would be up well before dawn, chanting their Pali recitations, and then, still prior to sunrise, they would be on their way to collect food for the day in their large metal bowls. They usually gathered more than enough, and knowing that I was vegetarian, they would give me extra rice, or a carton of milk, or similar food items.

My home was a one-room cement structure that had a small patio area with a concrete bench just outside the door. The vivid blue waters of the sea were a sheer drop of about 50 or 60 feet below and they stretched for miles to the distant horizon. This hermitage had originally been built by a monk who had used it as a haven from the busy world and then moved on. The place had been abandoned to wind and decay for quite a few years until I arrived. With the abbot's permission, I installed a new roof and moved in.

The most challenging aspect of life in this location was the distance to the temple proper – about one mile around the side of the hill overlooking the water. This was easy enough to walk in the daytime, but at night it was considerably more challenging, and there was also a very real risk of poisonous snakes on the trail. In some places, there was only bare rock sloping down to the ocean at a 45 degree angle, with small concrete stepping-places built into the rock surface.

One had to clamber from concrete step to concrete step sideways, something not difficult to do in full daylight, but quite challenging on moonless nights when visibility was greatly reduced.

Before long, the two monks who lived in the cave were joined by a third, younger monk who had a flair for asceticism. He moved his wooden bed-frame onto a precarious rock, thus creating a situation whereby if he ever rolled off his bed in the night, he would have a very bad and possibly fatal fall. The bed was somewhat insecurely lodged, and it looked like it might slide into the treetops at any time.

He did not speak English, so it was impossible to understand why he had made these arrangements, and difficult to imagine that they could last for very long. Before becoming a monk, this young man had been in a rock band in Chiangmai. Perhaps he felt that ascetic sleeping arrangements could loosen up and shuffle off some of his karma. Or he may have imagined that this form of penance could act as a curb on his desires. I never really understood his motives.

While living and meditating in my cell overlooking the sea, phases of insight and revelation would come and go. I had not yet clued in to one very significant fact: everything comes and goes. It's all impermanent. Moreover, what rises and falls is of necessity empty, and therefore not ultimately real.

The sound of the sea was incessant at the base of the cliff below my simple abode. The sun was bright and intense in the middle of the day. It was the dry season, so the tin roof soon became very hot. By early afternoon, the leaves on the trees were drooping and wilting in the heat of the motionless air. Day after day flowed by with the movement and the sound of wind and wave being the only natural elements to break the silence.

My new home in Thailand was a fixer-upper.

When I discovered this abandoned building, it needed a new roof. But once the abbot of the nearby temple gave his sanction and allowed me to live and meditate there, it was not hard to round up some helpers and make the place livable. The heat was such that the only way to work was with shirts off.

To the right of the doorway, you can see a bench where I would sometimes sit to meditate, either early in the morning or before going to sleep at night. In the area of the stone wall was another bench, not visible, where Lama Atal and I would meditate and converse.

The skies were sunny most of the time, and the afternoons were particularly hot. But the sound of the ocean waves nearby brought a feeling of harmony and depth to this simple abode. It probably would have been cooler and more airy in the building itself if I had not blocked in the windows with plywood, but this being my first experience of a tropical climate, I had much to learn.

7

Only The Ocean

Seated on the bench outside my hermitage, high above the Gulf of Siam, I could gaze on the eastern horizon each morning and see the first rosy rays of light tinge the skyline with radiance. The fading gray of the sky would slowly take on warm shades of pink and orange, and at last the sun would emerge from a point where sky and ocean seemed to meet. Then, the day would begin in earnest.

My visual landscape was utterly simplified. The fiery sun blazed in the air above, and the water of the ocean lapped against the rocks of the cliff below. The field of vision was reduced to just four elements: earth, water, fire and air. Somehow, this brought tranquility to the mind. During these long, peaceful days of almost unbroken solitude, thoughts of the busy world receded into insignificance.

One day, a monk wearing robes of dark burgundy arrived at the nearby cave and took up residence with the Thai monks, who typically wore robes of orange, or ochre. Within a day or two, he came over for a visit and offered me one or two items of food. To my delight, it turned out that he could speak perfect English!

Whereas the Thai monks used the prefix "Prah" in front of their individual names, this monk referred to himself as a "Lama", and it was not long before I heard him referred to by the Thai monks as "Lama Atal".

He would sometimes walk over from the cave and join me in silent meditation at sunrise. Often his approach and departure would be in silence, but from time to time we would chat.

I was interested to draw him out on the subject of meditation, and he asked about the kind of meditation that I was practicing.

One morning, when our silent contemplation of the sunrise had come to an end, he commented: "This is such a beautiful place to simply sit and be! Nature does the meditation on our behalf. Simplicity, beauty and the sound of the ocean – it could not be more perfect!"

I nodded agreement and added, "I've always felt that sunrise is a good time to meditate. Just watching the sun come up from the ocean seems to transport the mind into deeper stillness."

"It looks like the sun comes up from the water, doesn't it?" he replied.

"Well, of course it's millions of miles away in space," I answered. "But it appears to rise up from the ocean, I agree."

"Yes," he continued. "It's true, the way things appear and the way they really are can be so different. This is something to be aware of in our meditation, too."

"What do you mean?" I asked.

He paused as if bringing an understanding into clear focus.

"Close your eyes and listen for a moment," he said. "What do you hear?"

I closed my eyes. The sound of the ocean crashing against the rocks at the base of the cliff rose up to our ears. Slow and rhythmic, its cadence filled the air. "I hear the sound of the waves hitting against the stones at the base of the cliff," I replied.

"The waves?" he asked.

"Yes," I said.

I noticed that he remained silent for a long time. So I continued, "Why?"

"Think for a moment. What is a wave, actually?"

I thought the question was a bit odd. But I replied: "A wave is the ocean in movement, usually caused by wind on the ocean's surface."

"So, is a wave a "thing"?" he asked.

"I suppose so," I answered. "Well, now that you ask, I'm not sure."

"If I may ask another question," he continued. "Can there be any waves apart from the ocean?"

"No" I replied, with some measure of confidence.

"And on the other hand," he added, "can there be any ocean without waves?"

"I suppose there can be, on a calm day, at least" I replied, puzzled at where this line of questioning might be leading.

"So then, what are we to make of this?" he inquired, looking directly into my eyes.

"I'm not sure," I said. "Waves depend on the ocean, I guess."

"More than that," he asserted. "Much more than that. Waves are nothing more than a human notion superimposed on the ocean. No ocean, no waves."

"That seems clear enough," I replied. "Does this relate to meditation?"

"It does!" he asserted. "In reality, I mean, as things really are, beyond what we construe in our minds, there is no such thing as a wave. It simply does not exist until you make up a label and think of the ocean as a "wave".

"Oh, I see," I replied.

He cut me off abruptly. "Do you really see?"

He looked at me in silence. It felt awkward. I sensed he wantedto make an important point, but he hoped that I would see his point before he had to explain it.

"Well..." I began. "Well... I guess the point is that any given wave is only the ocean, but with a specific form and movement. But we imagine differently because we talk as if our words referred to real things."

"Indeed," he smiled. "And we meditate within this fabricated mindset which thinks of waves as something real when only the ocean is real. Can you see any implications of this?"

"Hmmm..." I paused for time. "Maybe "ocean" is only a conceptual designation itself?" I ventured.

"Maybe there is nothing at all beyond what we construe in our minds."

"And where does that get us?" he asked.

"Maybe if we stop thinking in words, in verbal labels, we would be closer to feeling or sensing what anything or everything actually is?" I asked, uncertain of my ground.

"Can we really know what anything is?" he asked.

"I'm not sure," I answered. I had crashed into an intellectual wall that I just could not see any way around. "I can't really say."

"And how does this state of unknowing feel?" he asked.

At this point, I began to suspect that he had a passing familiarity with New Age psychology, but I put that idea out of my mind.

Pausing for a while to listen to my feelings, I gazed eastward at the horizon and the newly risen sun.

"It doesn't really matter, as long as I don't think about it," I answered. "Everything is fine if I don't feel the need to verbalize. I mean, if I don't believe in words, then I don't believe stories built up from words either." A broad smile creased my face, and I turned to look him in the eyes again.

"That's it!" he said. And he smiled back. The sunlit cheer of his smile went straight into my heart.

"This," I commented to myself, "must be insight!"

"So, we can say," I went on, "that with regard to waves, there is only the ocean. Every wave, apart from being a mere label, is only the ocean. And beyond that, our conceptual notion about there being an ocean is not real either, except as a label or conjecture."

"More than that," he asserted. "We can say that apart from conceptual designations, there is only the unknowable. The labels are mental fantasy. Only the unknowable is real. But it can never be put into words."

"Real and unreal are themselves only notions," I commented. "Can the unknowable be experienced, then?"

"Yes, certainly," he stated. "But experiences come and go. They are like waves on the surface of the ocean, nothing but the ocean."

"Then, no one can grasp what is real with the mind," I ventured, "or at least not by means of words and concepts."

"You can try," he replied, "but all this thinking-activity does is to generate illusion. Our habit of saying "This is this" and "that is that" and then believing our labels and our stories is ignorance in action."

"So if we say that "there is only the ocean" we really mean that ultimately things are unknowable, and grasping at reality with labels and concepts is ignorance."

"Yes!" he asserted. "And I really hope you see this clearly."

"I'm guessing that this is what you meant when you said to factor this understanding into our meditation." I replied.

He smiled. We looked out across the ocean again. It was utterly calm.

After a few minutes of shared silence, he left.

The sun was higher above the horizon and the day was warming up by the minute.

"Only the ocean", I thought. "No labels, no ocean."

Then, I thought again: "What is real cannot be grasped with words. No concept, no problem."

"If there is no problem," I reflected, "there is no need to strive and struggle. Meditation won't make a wave more of the ocean. Reality has always been OK, just as it is."

More thoughts crowded in: "All I need to do is drop the noise in my mind. Forget the words. Forget the names. Forget the stories."

At this point, a feeling of elation arose that was quite new in my experience. "If there is no problem," I reasoned, "then there is no need to seek and strive for some kind of solution!"

I looked out over the ocean, and the sun was even higher in the sky.

"Well, I'm going to label this a good day!" At this point, I thought of some things that needed doing and returned to my customary "chop wood, carry water" routine.

8

Crossing The Ocean

My next conversation with Lama Atal was memorable. He described his own spiritual background and practice in clear and uncompromising terms.

"Traditionally," he began, "teachers take quite a few years to train their students in purification, self-discipline and transformation. They spent a lot of time modifying states of mind and developing other qualifications that would presumably result in enlightenment."

"But my approach is much more direct. In our essence," he continued, "we are already perfect, primordially liberated, requiring no transformation or improvement. This is called the "Great Perfection" in the Tibetan tradition, because it is without defects."

"So there is less need to strive?" I enquired, recollecting my conclusion of the previous day.

"There is no need to strive!" he affirmed. "The point is not to develop a whole new set of mental conditionings based on the ego's fascination with seeking, striving and attaining, but rather to come home to the perfection that is already present. It is as far or as close as the distance from the head to the heart."

"My own meditation has been heart-centered," I affirmed. "My teacher says that God is seated on his throne at the center of our hearts."

"Indeed," he affirmed, "everything we seek lies within us in the core of our own being. We need only return home to that part of our being where wisdom, love, creativity and all the other divine qualities are waiting to blossom. We bring the seeking mind home to the love, peace and light of the awakened heart, which is our true nature. Ultimately, the paths of discernment and surrender converge. Head and heart unite, love and wisdom merge, and the fulfilment of homecoming is complete."

"That is what I was taught too!" I exclaimed.

"All of this modification can be seen as the first stage of a long journey home, the journey from the egoic mind to the realization of the true Self," the lama continued. "But there is a more profound liberation, admittedly not for everyone."

"My guru insists that the path of the heart is the fastest and most effective path," I stated.

"Perhaps so, if you want to be a somebody who is going somewhere in a hurry," he mused. There was a wry expression on his face, the edges of his lips being lifted into a faint smile.

"What do you mean?" I asked.

"When we dream, the dream-character is absolutely real and vivid. But when we wake up, this character with whom we have been fully identified is seen to be only a mental fantasy," Lama Atal replied.

"It happens every night!" I agreed.

"Similarly, at some point, when the separate self, generated by our egoic mind, is seen to be a fantasy, the shift into a fully awakened state becomes possible." The lama stretched his arms and yawned. Then he paused and reflected.

"You wake up only when you stop sleeping," he added. "But not before."

"So, the shift from head to heart is not what it's all about?" I asked.

"The awakening process is as slow or as complicated as we choose to make it. You are under the impression that there is a doer, a practice and a goal. However, when the awakening dawns, it is clearly seen that no one goes anywhere, and *no one is either lost or saved.*" He punctuated this point by a quick glance.

"So the idea of becoming liberated is fantasy?" I asked.

"In the liberated state, the protagonist who keeps busy with his spiritual quests is seen to be a dream. Spiritual awakening transcends the dreaming state. Dreams end, clarity dawns, Reality outshines the fantasy. It's that simple."

"And this happens all at once?" I enquired.

"After an initial awakening," he replied, "there is a gradual freeing up of awareness from the need to strive, attain, progress and go somewhere in order to achieve something that was lacking. In the shift from awakening to full freedom from ignorance, the reality of being no-one and going nowhere becomes fully evident. The great perfection of everything and everyone becomes obvious, and it is a lived experience."

"So the whole literature of spiritual seeking is… is what?" I asked, with some sense of astonishment.

"Just a concession to the way things appear in our minds when we are getting ready to wake up," he smiled.

"But it's not how Reality really is," I asserted.

"Seeking, striving and attaining are perennial themes in the stories we create. But stories, beliefs and active projects, including spiritual ones, eventually outgrow their usefulness," he said, lowering his voice.

"They certainly do." I added, finding I had little to say.

"At some point, dreamers wake up, dreams dissolve, and reality reveals its essence." He gestured with his hands, turning them upward toward the rising sun.

"And there is no need to practice?" I asked.

"Apart from our inherited notions," he began, "there is no distant goal to seek and attain by striving or going elsewhere. Seeking is an activity of the ignorance, based on a misunderstanding of how things exist. It could never generate a "liberated seeker"."

"The seeker caught up in this kind of narrative is a dream character," I added.

"Projected by the subconscious mind," he completed the thought. "When this is seen and understood, everything changes," he said, standing up to go. "And yet, in one way also it all remains the same."

He left. I was alone again, no longer sure about anything, including the value of meditation. My meditation had largely been a form of striving, an activity of the ego, an enjoyment of altered states of consciousness.

I could see that the sun was rising higher in the sky. It looked like it was going to be another hot day.

Cliffside view of my abode.

This picture would have been taken at the very start of my sojourn beside the ocean. From the beach below, my retreat on the cliffside looks stark and open to the winds, but it was much more hospitable when you were actually there.

The long, hot afternoons, with so much sky and ocean all around, were preternaturally still. The afternoon heat was an especially drowsy time, but mornings and evenings were ideal for meditation.

I followed a custom which I had seen the monks carrying out faithfully on a daily basis, which was to acquire a small broom made of locally grown natural materials and sweep the floor and the patio once or even twice a day. Simple activities like carrying water from the far side of the hill, sweeping away leaves and dust, and sharing meals with monks in the nearby cave became elements of my daily routine.

The lack of amenities and distractions made it easier to remain in a contemplative mood than it would have been with electricity, a laptop computer, and visitors.

9

A View of the Ocean

As the weeks flew by in my eagle-nest above the ocean, I had many inner experiences and insights. Sometimes, experiences would come in the form of dreams, and at other times they would arise during or outside the times of formal, meditative sitting.

I recall one morning, sitting on my concrete bench overlooking the sea, having a powerful sensation of being flooded with love for all creation. This came quite uninvited, not triggered by any contrived prayer or meditation. I felt like a feather being carried downstream by a river on a wide current of love, a flow that was expansive, free and vast as the sky. It coursed through my entire being, revealing divine beauty in all I saw.

Here are some writings from that period of time:

Sky touches ocean
Along a horizon
My eye can see, but never reach.

Mind turns to spirit
Across a threshold
My thoughts can sense but never penetrate.

Agitation subsides into stillness
Within an infinity
My soul can feel, but never grasp.

My mind's commentary
And my outer involvement
Go hand in hand.

My mental notions
And my inner confusion
Are the same activity.

My teaching and my ignorance
Are an undivided whole.

My learning and my illusion
Are identical.

Silence, however does not separate,
And Silence does not discriminate.

By silence, the singleness of multiplicity
Is made apparent.

In silence the liberation from complexity
Becomes complete.

Stillness is the space,
Love the place,
Ego the experience,
Death the event,
Emptiness the revelation.
Emptiness is the space,
Emptiness the place,
Emptiness the experience,
Emptiness the event,
Fullness the revelation.

The knower unravels in the Unknowable,
The lover dissolves in love,
Desire subsides into peace,
And the wave returns at last to the ocean.

There is no object!

Silence has become the eloquence
Of that which is to be expressed –

The body of consciousness,
The mind of existence,
The heart of bliss,
The One beyond the many
Meditating ignorance into Himself.

10

A Temple By The Ocean

In the late afternoon, the monks at the Kao Takiap temple would come together for an extended session of chanting. My friend the abbot would sit at the front of the assembly and lecture them intermittently, smoking a cigarette now and then between discourses. I enjoyed sitting at the back of the hall and meditating to the sound of the Pali chants.

Within my first few weeks at the temple, I made the acquaintance of an elderly Buddhist nun who lived in a separate compound for women near the chanting hall. On one occasion, she made an effort to communicate with me through a friend who spoke both Thai and English.

She had watched me meditating as the monks chanted, and had seen a golden light around my body. She had also become aware of one of my inner guides, whom she had engaged in conversation. By thus observing my practice and conversing with this guide, she had gained some insight into my spiritual life which she was making an effort to share.

She told me that, according to Buddhism, the path to enlightenment had nine levels of achievement. At that time (1990) I was somewhere between the seventh and the eighth levels. She predicted that the work of starting a meditation center would prosper in time, but that it would be slow at first. She pointed to my blue star-sapphire ring, and said that it had a special significance for me.

I asked her what that was, but she said that I already knew. After that conversation, I never saw her again.

Before becoming a monk, the abbot of Wat Kao Takiap had been a wealthy Bangkok businessman, and his father had been the ambassador for Thailand to the United Kingdom. The father would visit the temple and stay with his son the abbot on weekends, with time out for golf. In many ways, life at this temple by the ocean was relaxed and easy-going with a perpetual stream of visitors, tourists, admirers and devotees.

One day, while digging in the temple garden, Luang-Paw Eed the abbot, to the great astonishment of all, unearthed a relic of the Lord Buddha! When he concentrated on this event, he came to understand that this relic had been teleported from Sri Lanka to the very spot where he had dug it up! At that same time, the local people and newspapers had noted a most unusual experience. A large flock of white bats had flown into the temple and then moved on and disappeared, something which had never happened before!

The matter-of-fact manner in which the abbot told me this story disarmed my initial credulity so that I was able to keep an open mind about the whole affair. In any case, the stories he told me were what he and the monks and the visitors all believed. The supporters' faith in the abbot and his spirituality was what made the temple a thriving center for Theravada Buddhism in that region of Southern Thailand.

From the time that the relic was discovered, quite a few cures and unusual phenomena began to happen in the temple. For example, photographs would show energy-lines and luminous globes in the air which had been invisible at the time of taking the photo. I was allowed to see a number of these snapshots in which unusual energy lines and floating spheres, suspended like soap bubbles in the air, were clearly visible.

At one point, I was asked by the abbot to re-arrange and decorate the altar where the Buddha relic was kept. There were dozens of statues of all sizes, gifts from devotees of the relic, resting on tables of differing heights. The relic of the Buddha was on display with no special security system in place to protect it, which I found surprising.

I remember the abbot explaining that word of this relic had reached Sri Lanka. Some devotees there had contacted the abbot to ask if they could have the precious relic back, on loan, for a while. The abbot confided to me that after receiving this request he had travelled to Sri Lanka in his astral body to evaluate their sincerity, and had then decided against the request on the basis that they were not persons of integrity.

The monks who lived at Wat Kow-Takiap were firmly convinced that their leader, whom they affectionately called "Paw-Eed", or "father Ed", had special powers to bless and heal and to see the invisible and occult side of things.

I had no reason to doubt them, although I did not know what to make of the miracles and the discovery of this remarkable relic.

When one lives in Thailand, one encounters a very different mindset and cultural background from that in the United States or Canada. The presence of spirits, especially nature spirits, is universally believed. There is a spirit house in virtually every home and business, and flowers, incense and food offerings are regularly placed in these spirit houses to win the favour of the invisible helpers. Quite a few people I talked to had seen ghosts, apparitions and nature devas and they were afraid of being alone in the dark, or anywhere near a graveyard after sunset.

One of my discoveries from this period of time was the Vissudhi-Magga, a classic Buddhist text on meditation. This book describes the deepening stages of meditation in terms of four *jhanas*. The word "*jhana*" is a Pali term referring to deep states of contemplative absorption. It was a great joy to read descriptions of the four *jhanas* and correlate them with my own inner experience. I had never seen the stages of meditative absorption described so clearly, convincingly, and (to the extent that it matched my own experience) so meaningfully.

Now, at last, I had a definitive map of how contemplative experience unfolds. It was of the very highest reliability and quite free of cultural or religious baggage such as guru-worship. It confirmed my own experience that "letting go" is at the very heart of the contemplative journey.

In the *jhana* teachings, the meditator notices the imperfection, delusion, or un-satisfactoriness (dukka) of his or her current state of awareness and releases all attachment whatsoever to that state of mind. This is another way of saying that *the meditator drops all sense of identification with the current contents of consciousness as they arise into the conscious mind. This act of letting go is what liberates. The key point is that there is no need to hanker after what will come next, as this letting go is not a form of striving for something better, and there is no sense of grasping for a different or enhanced quality of experience.*

One simply lets go of the current contents in the field of awareness and opens the mind and heart to the ineffable.

My experience in meditation had long been that opening the spiritual heart speeds the transition from a lower to a higher *jhana*. The higher *jhanas* are experienced as being suffused with bliss, peace and equanimity in progressively deepening measure. Of course, letting go is something that we can do with our minds. But opening up from the heart, which is the affective and intuitive center of the being, is a different process. When we activate our deepest capacity for selfless love, devotion and intuitive attunement, the unknowable is sensed to be a living presence.

Taken together, letting go and opening up are the essence of the contemplative journey from samsara to nirvana, and from suffering to joy.

As my meditative retreat by the ocean moved through days into weeks and months, daily meditations deepened and I could intuit these processes at work in the rising and falling of the ocean's waves. Rising up, a wave opens its form to the empty sky above. Letting go, the wave subsides into the sea again. The oceanic power and presence moves in and through its numberless wave-forms, opening them up and letting them go continuously.

This is recognized more easily if one can see from the heart, with the *eyes of the heart*. One way of explaining how to open up the heart is simply to laugh or smile. If we can do lots of that, the opening will come more easily. Alternately, if you remember a time when you were listening to music so beautiful that it brought tears to your eyes, then also you can locate your deepest feelings in the domain of the spiritual heart.

The opening of the heart is always a homecoming to something felt to be peaceful and blissful, centering and complete. Letting go at the level of the mind is also always an experience of release whether it be of an attitude or judgment, a feeling, or any kind of identification.

That which the mind sees and experiences as *emptiness* is directly known and felt by the heart as *fullness*. This inner fullness can be experienced as peace, or as bliss or as love or as profound equanimity – indeed, it has many facets. Most simply expressed, the heart opens to the Divine, or to Truth, or to the Light, or to infinite Love, which are felt and intimately known in a most direct and immediate way.

11

Notes From The Ocean

In the journal of insights and experiences that I wrote down during these weeks of meditation near the ocean, the following stand out:

Thought is always based on the notion of a separate perceiving self and its grasping. Thinking never subsists, never enters the state of profound peace by itself, because its impetus is the ego-motive, and ego is unwilling to die.

But ego-death and liberation are inseparable. Therefore, the degree of letting go must be ultimate and complete.

When the wave subsides into the ocean, it forgets its form and its sense of separation. Then comes the liberating insight that it was always and only the water of the ocean. Big waves are not wetter then small ones. None of them are at any moment anything other than the ocean.

Based as it is on the distorted ego-notion and depending as it does on changeable appearances, the thinking activity of the mind can embrace only greater or lesser degrees of ignorance. It cannot conform to the truth of its being unless it subsides into the heart.

The egoic mind never survives the dawn of liberation. It simply ceases its confused seeking and lets go of its separate existence. No ego is ever liberated. Seeking- activity comes to an end and the egoic wave-form merges in the ocean of infinite peace.

In the silent state, one clearly sees that there is no "I" and no "other". If mind can step beyond its egoic motivations and be free of the movement of thought, it can experience its existence as none other than the Ocean of Being.

This is Peace and this is Release. This is Liberation.

Khao Takiap, with bay and beach.

This photo of Khao Takiap was taken in 1990, when the area was relatively peaceful and undeveloped. Modern photos show that it has since become a tourist magnet with upscale hotels and shops.

When I arrived to this area, Kaho Takiap's natural beauty had been largely undisturbed. The pristine combination of ocean, mountain, sky and wind made it a perfect place to meditate and gain firsthand experience with the Jhanas.

Wat Khao Takiap, a Theravada Buddhist Monastery, was situated on the far side of this hill. My simple hermitage was situated about a mile away from the Monastery, on a ledge overlooking the waters of the gulf of Siam. But getting to and from the Monastery was not an easy walk. One had to carefully traverse forested hillsides and rocky ledges overlooking the sea.

One dark evening, when the monks who lived in a nearby cave returned from the far side of Khao Takiap, they described narrowly missing a poisonous snake bite when stepping over a fallen log. Although there were natural hazards like this in the area, and I had to deal with one or two scorpions within my shelter, I felt quite safe.

12

The Song of the Ocean Waves

Several months after I arrived in Thailand, a Buddhist monk gave me a small piece of bone from the funeral pyre of an "arhat", a monk who had attained full liberation, or as he called it, "pani- nippan". I bought a heart-shaped silver locket and chain and wore this relic inside the locket. The length of the chain was such that the relic hung directly over my heart.

Sometimes, when I was in a meditative mood, I would try to feel a connection with the consciousness of this liberated being.

"Who are you?" I would ask.

"And who am I?" I would continue.

I would wait for an answer.

One day, an answer came, in the form of a question: "The wave asks the ocean, "Who am I?"

It felt like a further question was being implied: "Does this even make sense?"

The silence that followed was charged with an energy or presence that I could not explain or describe.

At other times, when that same presence would come back again, like a high-pitched humming in the air, I would say to myself, "This is Presence." And so the need for using words to grasp experiences continued.

When I would sit and watch the distant horizon from my bench over-looking the Gulf of Siam, I could hear the ocean waves singing to me incessantly of the eternal cosmic flow.

"Presence," the waves would sing. "Hear the Presence."

Day and night their rhythm continued. Sometimes, when the wind was strong, the waves would crash violently upon the cliffs below. On other days, when there was no breeze at all, the waves would subside and there would be the ocean, only the ocean, perfectly reflecting the stars and the moon high above in the night-time sky.

Alone in my small hut, I would sometimes breathe through my nostrils so that the breath would make a sound not unlike the sound of the ocean's waves on the back of my palate. "Opening Up," I would think with each long, slow, deep inhalation. And "Letting Go," I would feel with each gentle exhalation.

Then, as the space between breaths gradually became prolonged, and as I relaxed into deeper mental stillness, I would feel the ocean of life flowing through the body. Its endless cycle of opening up and letting go was the very source of my breath. Its life was my life. How could there possibly be any separations of reality into "this" and "that", except by way of verbal labels? More and more, inner silence became a refuge of immersion in Presence.

At times, when I was very still, my breath having virtually come to a stop, I could feel the pulse of my heartbeat as it sent waves of blood through the rivulets of my veins and life-energy flowing in the cells of the body.

And I would sometimes wonder: "How and why is this mystery as it is? It is so strange that any of this appears in this way."

One morning when Lama Atal visited me for sunrise meditation, I felt it was time to ask the question which had been forming itself at the back of my mind for several days.

"Why," I asked, "is the ocean so inspiring? I feel it is so good to live and meditate close to the ocean. Why is that?"

"The ocean," he began, "is alive and conscious, vast and powerful. Our bodies are mostly water, and this water flows rhythmically in us as it does in the ocean. We exist in the cosmic flow, according to its rhythms. It is the flow of life, love and creative power for the planet and for us equally. The ocean is our ancient mother."

"Ahh, that says it all," I replied. "There is a call to come home to the Mother."

"But look beyond this ocean. Look up into the skies at night. The cosmos is a great ocean of flowing energy," he went on. "Just as water can solidify into pieces of ice, the cosmic energy can crystallize into physical forms such as planets and people. Ice is still water, and physical forms are this very cosmic energy in solid form."

"In the Heart Sutra," I said, "the Buddha teaches that form is empty and that emptiness is form."

"Just so, isn't it!" he replied, in a way that struck me as quaint. "But our minds are programmed by our use of language and we do not notice how things really are. We name objects in various ways, and then we believe they are something other than waves of the cosmic ocean. They are all of the same essence, the same taste. But just as the ocean's waves are impermanent, so are objects. They all rise and fall in the tides of eternity."

He paused and looked out over the Gulf of Siam, shading his eyes with his right hand. "So there is an ocean beyond this physical ocean that you hear calling to you. It is the cosmic ocean of life and energy behind everything that appears. When we live near the waters of this physical ocean, we can feel the resonance of something invisible. Invisible, but vast, isn't it?"

I noticed his use of the phrase "isn't it", and wondered if he had lived in Malaysia, where I had heard this expression beingused in just this way.

Lama Atal paused again and then continued: "Cosmos is not merely "behind" everything that appears, it IS everything that appears. It is all what we could call the body of God. In this sense, all things are sacred and good in their very essence.

We Tibetans refer to this as "Samantabhadra", or "Great Perfection". As complicated humans, however, we sometimes experience life as suffering."

He paused yet again. "But perfection is how existence really is."

"I can feel this when I live by the ocean," I ventured. "In the city, not so much."

"We sense the cosmic flow, and we instinctively feel that we are part of this flow. Or we can feel that the cosmic flow is our real identity, even though it is not something we can grasp. Once this is realized, the door opens to full enlightenment."

"Liberation means the letting go of what we are not, and enlightenment means opening up to the fullness of what we really are, isn't it?" I played with the phrase, observing whether he would notice this playfully imitative turn of phrase.

"This is the only way to be as you really are," he replied. "The song of the ocean waves is a song of opening up and letting go, yes indeed. It is the rhythmic pulse of the cosmic life. You are that. You are only that. You are not anything you have imagined or believed. This is known and experienced directly in deep contemplation."

He paused and looked at me intently.

"However.."

"However?" I asked.

"However, saying this kind of thing does not mean we are actually realizing it. There is a big difference between talk and realization, or direct experience."

"But isn't it a step in the right direction, at least, to speak these truths?" I asked.

"For whom?" he asked.

"For the one who is seeking the truth!" I asserted, with a sense of stating the obvious.

"Does the wave need to seek the ocean?" He looked out over the ocean.

Then he looked at me directly and stated: "Every wave, until conceptualized, is only the ocean, free of confusion, just *BECAUSE it is not looking elsewhere!"*

The statement powerfully impacted my mind, and I shifted into a state of inner stillness as I slowly began to reply. "You are saying that the activity of spiritual seeking keeps the ignorance in place?" My voice was tinged with disbelief.

"Waves ARE the ocean," he asserted. "Ignorance is a mere label." This leap of logic baffled me. Then, I saw the light.

"Yes, I see it now! The idea that a wave needs to look for the ocean is indeed foolish. There is no such thing as a wave, there is only the ocean. And certainly there is no such thing as "an ignorant wave", only the ignorant activity of conceptualizing something separate from the ocean."

Lama Atal smiled. And again, it was like the sun coming out from the clouds. In my heart, there was a burst of joy. I resisted the impulse to grasp and label it. Lama stood up, paused, smiled again, and left in silence.

Tranquil spot by the bay with Hua Hin in the background.

This photo of me was taken on the side of Khao Takiap which is situated nearest to the tourist city of Hua Hin, seen in the background. A giant Buddha statue had recently been erected on the cliffs overlooking the Gulf of Siam and loomed several stories high on the landscape.

The youngest monks, who were still basically children, would sometimes enjoy swimming in this bay. Thai visitors of all ages would arrive at the temple and wander its grounds, day in and day out, pausing to burn sticks of incense at certain shrines, or laying out a picnic when the time came to relax.

The royal family had a palace several miles north of Hua Hin, with extensive beachfront real estate, and this was what put Hua Hin on the map back in the day. By the mid 1980's, Hua Hin had been discovered by tourists and land developers, and was quickly being turned into a tourist mecca.

My hermitage on the far side of Wat Kao Takiap had the simplicity and peace of pre-tourist Thailand, and was a world apart from the madding crowds of Hua Hin.

13

The Ineffable Ocean

"You have the impression," Lama Atal began, "that spiritual attainment is a matter of knowing."

This caught my attention. I turned my head quizzically and glanced in his direction.

"Anything you can put into words," he continued, "is trivial. Enlightenment is unknowing."

"Can you explain?" I asked.

"Look out at the ocean, and the skyline and the sky," he said, pointing eastward. "Look at the vastness and the beauty. What do you gain by framing this in words and concepts?"

"I suppose," I hesitated, "that much of my understanding of spirituality has come through words and books, so I see books and words as repositories of spiritual knowledge."

"I know that you think this way," he replied. "That is why I am saying this. One master with whom I studied put it this way: 'Do not suppose that what you attain becomes your knowledge and is grasped by your intellect. Although actualized immediately, what is inconceivable may not be apparent. Its emergence is beyond your knowledge,' I memorized that passage because it corrected a misunderstanding that I brought to the path when I first started."

"The path is always being described by words in books," I began.

He cut me off. "And yet the activity of reading is nothing short of dualistic amnesia."

He paused for me to reply, but I had nothing to say.

"Looking at a photograph of this scene before us could not compare with the living reality, could it?" he asked, waving his arm towards the seascape.

"No," I replied. "No, it certainly couldn't."

"How much less, then, could words on a page do justice to the condition of enlightenment!"

"True," I admitted.

"Or dots and dashes, as in Morse Code?" he went on, extending the metaphor. "How much of life's magic can these things actually convey?"

"Well, people feel this need to know with their minds," I ventured.

"And this kind of intellectual grasping prolongs their ignorance," he stated. "Does the wave need to study the nature of the ocean? Is it not enough to just BE the ocean, and rise and fall with the cosmic flow?"

"I suppose that this should be enough," I answered. "But…

"The thinking activity of the mind keeps the ego alive, and so it creates a big research project and a set of practices for this express purpose. First the very elaborate practices, then the elaborate ones, then the basic practices and then the abbreviated ones, and then…"

I felt frustration in his voice, as if he had been through this process himself, and discovered its futility first-hand.

"… then the highly abbreviated practices. And then the manuals to study, first the elaborate ones, then… well, you get the picture."

"I guess Lama-studies are complicated," I sighed.

He smiled, as if catching himself in the act of ranting.

"Letting go is all we need," he replied. "That, and opening up."

"I know the nature of the ocean cannot be captured in any set of verbal labels," I admitted, "even if they are pith teachings."

"And yet, you want to write the "Great Liberation Sutra!" he laughed.

I laughed too. But he had very accurately exposed my motivations. I wanted to say what was worth saying about what was most important, and in the best way possible. I saw, in this moment, that the urge to know and to verbalize was indeed an act of grasping. Under the guise of spiritual utility, it was actually, at a certain stage in the journey, an obstacle to the process of full awakening.

"The need to know, the need to say, the need to write, the need to grasp reality by means of verbal statements – it will all come to an end," he predicted. "Every windy day is followed by a period of calm. It is inevitable."

Again, he looked out toward the horizon. The sun was setting behind us, and the sky had a beautiful subtlety of colour that I had rarely seen before.

"You know," I joked, "there IS a book in all of this!" We both laughed.

"I want to ask you for the first autographed copy," he joked.

"Done!" I promised.

That said, Lama Atal headed back to the cave where the other monks were getting ready for the last meal of the day.

* * * * * *

On this particular night, on the point of falling asleep, I took my silver locket in my right hand, and tried to make contact with the consciousness of the arhat whose body had yielded up the bone it contained.

I visualized the atomic structure of the bone as a cosmic ocean of infinite light and energy. Then, I melted into that sea of light and let go of all sense that I even existed as a separate being. I became a formless flow of indescribable vastness.

In that moment, releasing all need or interest to know and grasp with words, I could actually feel that immersion in the cosmic flow was more than enough. In any case, it clearly beggared description. Of this I was sure.

The experience sank into the depths of my psyche, and I fell asleep.

A visit with Luang Paw Eed.

One of the most influential and respected monks I came to know in Thailand was Luang Paw Eed. This photo gives you an idea of Luang Paw Eed's living arrangements. He had a constant stream of visitors, most of whom would make a contribution to the temple in currency or kind.

You could say that Luang Paw Eed was a VIP in that part of the world. He and my Indian Guru had become friends, and so Paw Eed was happy to help me get started on my assignment, which was to start a meditation center. His English was excellent, and this made him one of the few people who could help me facilitate this task.

Most of the monks believed that Paw Eed had special spiritual and occult powers, and I witnessed the reverence with which they would approach him for blessings or for approval to undertake specific spiritual practices.

Over time, quite a few bronze Buddha statues had accumulated because of the generosity and devotion of his visitors. These offerings surrounded an ancient Buddha Relic on an altar. The Relic itself had been obtained through a miraculous discovery on temple grounds.

One day, Paw Eed asked me to rearrange all of the statues on the altar where the Buddha Relic was kept. I was honored to be allowed to touch these devotional objects, and in the small act of rearranging them, share a part of their history.

14

The Triple Ocean

Typically, Lama Atal and I would meet on my patio overlooking the ocean, meditate in silence and then share breakfast after our silent meditation had ended. The peace and depth of our regular morning meditations was growing day by day.

Lama Atal's background was Mahayana rather than Theravada, like the Thai monks. And within the Mahayana lineage, he was a Nyingma master, known as a "Rinpoche", or "precious jewel".

This is a title indicating real spiritual attainment. He was not a monk, and so he was at liberty to marry and become a householder whenever he wanted, and still retain the title of "Rinpoche." However, I felt he enjoyed his many freedoms and his peripatetic lifestyle, and that for him, life was good just as it was.

"I meditated on your question the other evening," Lama Atal mentioned, "and I wanted to share one or two more points about why you feel this way about the ocean."

"Oh," I said, "Please sit down, and we can chat."

"I spoke about water being part of the cosmic flow," he began, as he sat on the bench and arranged his robes. "And physical objects are like ice-cubes, or crystallizations within that flow. But I did not explain that there are actually three oceans, all of which you embody. So the closeness you feel to the ocean really arises from being aware of the truth of your being."

"I do feel that I am somehow "at home" when living near the ocean," I replied. "Astrologically, I have four planets in the sign of Cancer which is a water sign. Maybe that helps explain it. But can you tell me more about these three oceans?"

"The first ocean is physical, and the oceans of Mother Earth are the water element within that ocean. The second ocean is the energetic mandala behind physical appearances. The third ocean is ineffable emptiness, the ground of being in which the other oceans appear and interact. Infinite consciousness is the radiance of the unknowable ground of being. But the ground of being is impossible to describe."

"In my studies, I have come across the expression, "light of consciousness," I replied. "And I have also read about an ultimate reality called Sat-Chit-Ananda. Becoming fully conscious is sometimes equated to being 'enlightened'."

"The individual is a wave that arises and recedes in the triple ocean of existence," Lama Atal continued. "The physical ocean abides in the ocean of light. Consciousness is simply the radiance of the ineffable. In Tibet, they speak of three kayas, the Nirmanakaya, which is the physical, the Sambhogakaya, which is the luminosity of consciousness, sometimes called "Presence", and the Dharmakaya which is ineffable. Pure awareness is sometimes called the clear light of the Dharmakaya."

"It all sounds like spiritual cosmology," I replied. "But really, it's just a way of talking about who and what we really are. Am I right?"

"It is a way of talking about the cosmos and its flow," Lama Atal replied. "Transcendent reality is beyond manifestation, so we have little to say about it. We can talk about the cosmos, but when we conceptualize "things" we get side-tracked. So let's think in terms of process or flow."

"I feel," I added, "that the ocean constantly calls and pulls me toward something vast and profound. The waves of the ocean move in and out of form, ceaselessly. They seem to call me home. An ancient home beyond anything I know or can describe."

"That is true," he commented. "The ocean exists in a state of constant flow, empty of form in itself, but always moving into and out of form. It expresses the cosmic flow in a way we can see and feel."

"In many ways, that is also how we arise and appear," I said. "In terms of being a human, it's the largest part of how we ARE."

"Not quite," he corrected me. "The part of us that appears is a small fraction of who and what we are. Our essence is immeasurable, indescribable. We make it very small when we reduce it to something that can be discussed. It is like talking about the greatness of love in terms of inches or centimeters."

Lama Atal had a gift for making things things clear and simple. I could feel that he spoke from his heart, and so my heart was wide open to what he was sharing. I felt that he was an ideal spiritual friend, generous with his time, not seeking any reward, kind and helpful, consistently clear and cogent with his teachings.

"But all of this is just talk!" he suddenly blurted out. "It adds up to nothing. Nothing at all!"

I stared at him in surprise.

"Look," he said. "You are either a slave, or you are free. It's as simple as that. In your case, you are a slave. Who knows if that will ever change!"

My surprise flipped instantly into shock.

"I'm saying that you are a slave to your mind, your thinking activity. Either you control it, or it controls you. It is that simple. If you imagine otherwise, then the onus is on you to prove your case."

"What do you mean?" I asked.

"If you are not the slave of your mind, then turn it off. Stop thinking. If you can do this, you are liberated. If you can't, you are a slave. Show me you aren't a slave."

With this, he got up and walked away toward the cave.

I could not believe that he had suddenly altered in this way. But he had. I was reminded of the quirky and sometimes harsh behavior that Don Juan occasionally displayed to Carlos Castaneda, and I recalled that his surprises had always served a good purpose.

Lama Atal had challenged me to stop thinking. So this is what I had to do.

It was not easy. I quickly learned that turning off the mind was not something I could just "do". To get into this state of being, I had to learn to relax. Just simply being, resting as being, as you allow the mind to let go, let go, let go of topics – that was the challenge!

Before long, I found myself slipping into meditative states of different kinds. The consciousness would feel very peaceful, then it would feel blissful. Then it would come into a condition of great stillness.

"Perhaps," I thought, "this is the liberated state."

Then I would let go of that thought, remind myself that it was a kind of slavery, and make a note to ask Lama Atal, if I ever saw him again. And so it went for several days.

15

Pointing Out The Ocean

To my great joy, Lama Atal rejoined me at our morning meditation a few days after his challenge. I was looking forward to sharing my experiences with him, and he must have sensed it.

The sun was well above the eastern horizon when our meditation came to an end. We sat for a while with our eyes closed. Then I heard his voice.

"Well?" he said.

"I did it," I replied.

"Did what?" he asked.

"I proved to myself that I'm not the slave of my mind."

"How did you do that?" he inquired.

"I turned it off. I stopped thinking. I can do it at will now. It was not easy at first, but I've found a way that works."

"And no thoughts come to you?" he asked, turning to look at me.

I sensed from his action that this was a critical point. I paused, in an effort to be absolutely correct and truthful with my answer.

"Thoughts come," I said. "But I don't follow them. I notice them, and just let them go. Letting go and relaxing are the key. That's my experience."

"That is fine!" he said with a smile, with the same effect as always. I felt that I was more fully alive when the radiance of his heart poured out through his eyes.

"I slip into meditative states of peace and bliss," I said proudly, thinking to please him.

Suddenly the smile disappeared from his face. "Is that bad?" I asked, with concern.

"This is still mental content," he stated. "You can be a slave to this kind of thing just as easily as you can to thoughts."

I was truly shocked to hear this. And it must have shown.

"A meditative state counts as a topic," he declared. "You get absorbed in these temporary states and they fill in the spaciousness of your awareness."

"Oh…" I said, crestfallen.

"Look," he continued. "I want to ask you one simple question, and I want you to answer it carefully and accurately. When your mind is without a topic, what is your experience?"

I switched into to a topic-less mind, allowing the mind to rest thought-free for some minutes. Then I turned to him and said: "It's not nothing. And at the same time, it's not a "thing". Beyond that, I find it hard to say…."

"Exactly!" he asserted. Again, that smile.

"You seem pleased," I said, with a touch of hesitancy.

"You have recognized what we Tibetans call rigpa - empty awareness, thought-free, relaxed presence. It is very simple. It is not more than that. That is the nature of mind. That is the nature of the ocean."

"But it is something very ordinary," I said.

"Indeed," he continued smiling.

"It's not meditation." I stated. "It's not peaceful, blissful, or loving."

"No," he agreed. "It derives from non-meditation, in fact. There is no striving and no doing involved. It's just plain and simple conscious being, no doing, no doer. It's not very… entrancing, is it?"

"Well, no…" I replied, reflecting on his choice of words.

"So now, I want you to continue on like this when you practice. Just relax into a truly thought-free mind, a mind with no topics, no special states. I'll see you again tomorrow."

"One more thing," he added. "And this is a quote from my master that I memorized. I felt it was worth the time to commend this point to memory, just as I read it."

"May I write it down?" I asked.

"Yes, by all means," he nodded. I took dictation as he spoke.

Lama Atal's words were enunciated slowly and clearly, as if he were engraving them on a tablet: "Realize the fictional nature of ALL your mind's conceptual constructs. See clearly that all subjects and objects are fictional, conceptual constructs that only exist in the mind. Let go of your conceptual constructing. Suffering arises only from the fictional stories that we weave in our thoughts. Apart from our notions and narratives, no causes of suffering actually exist. Nirvana is simply the absence of all conceptual constructions, the cessation of such fictional daydreaming."

"Is that clear?" he asked.

"Very clear," I replied.

He continued: "There is an ongoing storyline in your mind about being a "seeker" who strives to be better and who believes he can attain Buddhahood by accumulating positive energy and experiences. All the various forms of spiritual striving are expected to help this individual become free of suffering and get liberated. But this is like believing one is actually the character who appeared in last night's dream. The person and the dream are all contrived fantasy."

"I have it written down," I said

"If you have understood what it means, then you can paraphrase it in your own words," he smiled. "Can you do that for me, please?"

"Well..." I began slowly. "The wave has the sense of being other than the ocean, but it believes that it can achieve the status of the ocean if it strives and struggles. This results in various practices and techniques which are repeated over and over."

"Correct!" he pronounced.

"This situation of imagining that the wave is other than the ocean is only a dream. It is all mental delusion. Consciousness imagines itself to be individualized and distinct from the empty ocean of Dharmakaya. That is why the struggle and the striving are ignorance. They forget that the wave IS the ocean. Always has been. Always will be. End of fantasy. End of storyline. Full stop."

"And?" he queried.

"And pointing out the nature of mind makes it clear that this is not so. The pointing out experience is a recognition that wave is ocean. One continues on in this recognition, and this is called "non-meditation."

"There you are! You have it!" he smiled. I smiled too.

"At least, intellectually…" he added.

My smile faded.

"But this is still a very good step in the right direction!" he ventured, with a note of optimism in his voice.

And with that, he left.

16

The Blissful Ocean

The following morning, when our meditation ended, we resumed our conversation.

"I find that meditative states of peace and bliss keep coming back and I feel inclined to slip into them and just rest in a blissful, thought-free state," I admitted.

"Is this bliss a permanent state, or is it rather something that comes and goes?" he asked.

"It comes and goes," I replied.

"Then, would you call it the ocean or the wave?" he continued.

"I suppose it's the wave," I confessed.

"But what is the important thing to remember about waves, do you remember?" he queried me.

"Every wave is always and only the ocean," I replied. "So what is the problem with being a wave, then, if it's only the ocean, and the ocean is what is real?"

"This brings us to an important point," he began. "And it's one that we must be clear about. We are always and only liberated consciousness. Sometimes we do not recognize this fact and we have interactions with impermanent appearances. At other times, we recognize the truth of our situation.

But in every case the forms which appear to our mind are no more different from our true nature than the wave is from the ocean."

"Does this make a difference for the way we meditate?" I asked. "What do we need to do or not do?"

"If you abide in bliss, you either recognize your pristine awareness nature or you do not. If you do not, that is samsara and samsara is suffering. If you do, that is nirvana, and nirvana is liberation."

"We are always rigpa, in any case!" I challenged him.

"There is no "we," he countered. "The wave is only the ocean."

"The choice is to be conscious of who we really are, or to be unconscious," I ventured. "I choose to be conscious," I continued. "So again, what do I do, or not do when I sit to meditate?"

"Just remember, the ocean does not need to do anything to be the ocean. Nor does the wave." Lama Atal focused his attention on me, as if making a key point. "In non-meditation, you allow experiences of all kinds and thoughts of all kinds to arise and pass. Take no interest in them. Recognize spaciousness, the true nature, and just let go, let go, let go. Relax. Simply be. But do this without any conscious intent. Just do it naturally. It is the simplest thing in the world, and for that reason perhaps not so easy as you might think."

"I hear what you are saying, Lama Atal," I began. "I really believe I do. But I know where my difficulty will lie."

"I think I do too," he said with an especially gentle tone of voice. "But tell me anyway."

"I am afraid that sitting to meditate will become boring."

"Now we come down to the crux of the matter, don't we? Is that the expression, 'crux of the matter'?" he chuckled.

"I guess so," I replied, remembering that English was probably his second language, although he spoke it fluently.

"As long as the wind blows," he began, "there will be waves on the surface of the ocean. The winds whip up the hunger for experience, and the hunger for experience will find many ways to keep you busy. The higher the waves rise, due to the wind, the deeper they subside when they merge in their Source."

"That is so true," I commented.

"You know, a time will come when your interest in various kinds of experience will exhaust itself. Even a small taste of pure rigpa now and then will dilute the hunger that leads your mind into busyness. You will find that, if you continue to take some time each day and simply be as you are, you will quickly come home to the way of naturally and effortlessly abiding in the real."

"And… the wave will merge in the ocean," I added.

"Yes, that is what I mean," he admitted.

"And that is a better way of saying it, since the ocean is empty of waves and of "you" and of home and homecoming and other concepts and labels. The ocean does not create labels or believe in stories either. But yes, the wave subsides in the ocean, and that is a good way to put it."

"Should I reject thoughts and meditative states, then?" I asked.

"No need," he replied, "unless they preoccupy your mind and pull you away from the knowledge that they are waves and you are the ocean. Just don't follow them, take an interest in them, elaborate them, or believe them. That is enough."

"This is wisdom!" I murmured admiringly.

"Love and blessings," he replied, standing up. We folded hands and bowed our heads to each other.

Then, he turned and walked away.

I looked out to the eastern horizon where the sky touched the ocean, and felt a breeze moving in from the east. There were clouds in the sky, and I sensed that rain might be on the way. The sun was hidden behind the clouds, but the earth was hungry for the moisture that the rain would bring.

I decided to tidy my cabin and return to the wisdom that had just been pointed out. I decided to allow the waves while remembering the ocean, but not by dint of concentrated effort.

Simply by relaxing and letting go, I released each and every wave as it arose. In this way, I opened up to the fullness of the ocean.

As I passed through the doorway into my simple shelter, I reminded myself that even this degree of conscious intent was something to release. Letting go of the thought of letting go, I began to fold the bedding and prepare to sit for non-meditation. There was a small scorpion under the grass mat where I slept.

I removed him from the cabin with surprising calm. Once seated, I breathed in slowly and deeply through the nostrils. Exhaling, I relaxed.

Continuing in this way, I allowed the space between breaths to lengthen, and the feeling of peace to deepen. Letting go of my awareness of breathing, I entered a state of objectless shamatha. It was heart-centered rather than head-centered. The bliss was there, as usual.

I allowed it to be. I let go of allowing. The inexpressible spaciousness alone was real.

When the meditation ended, I penned these words:

Drop into the still point of the heart,
Let the mind release and unwind all on its own.
Rest as the observing still point
In the very center of the turbulent whirling,
Where no seeker can ever be found,
And no seeking-activity occurs.
The seeking self and the turbulence will vanish
Naturally, completely, all on their own!
The wave of separation seeking its home
Will sink into the ocean of being,
And the peace of non-striving alone will prevail.

17

Written On Water

"Remember," Lama Atal said, "A wave is a process, not a thing. It is a movement of the ocean, a flow. Each wave moves through the same stages, and each returns to its source."

"What are these stages?" I asked.

"You tell me," he replied.

I paused to think. "Well," I began, "Firstly, the wave arises up from the ocean itself."

"Yes," he asserted. "And this arising increases the surface area of the ocean. It brings the ocean into contact with more air and more light."

"Then," I continued, "the wave sinks back into the ocean."

"Before that happens," Lama Atal corrected me, "the wave releases its upward momentum. And this release leads directly to the next phase, which is…. ?"

"The wave subsides," I replied.

"Exactly," he replied. "So, we have three stages, right?"

The look in his eye suggested that he was not inviting agreement so much as insight. And yet, I could not see how it was possible to add anything to his tidy, three-part exposition.

"I get the feeling that there is something else I'm missing," I admitted.

"Once the wave has subsided," Lama Atal prompted me, "there is no wave, is there?"

"Was there ever a wave?" I asked, remembering our earlier talks. "I mean, apart from the ocean itself, which was temporarily in movement, what could a wave possibly be?"

"Yes, at all stages, whether arising, releasing or subsiding, what we called a wave was only the ocean in movement, indeed," he agreed. "And yet, when the wave has subsided, what remains of the wave?"

"The ocean," I replied, with a sense of stating the obvious.

"The ocean, of course," he admitted. "But when waves have all subsided, the ocean is no longer "waving", is it?"

"No," I agreed. "It has stopped moving."

"The ocean is always the ocean, whether it is rising, releasing, subsiding or ....."

He looked at me meaningfully, waiting for completion of his thought.

"Resting," I said. His nod assured me that this was the answer he had anticipated.

"It is all written on water," Lama Atal continued. "No wave has or is anything in itself, except the ocean's movement. Why would the ocean move? The wind of desire, a certain hunger for experience, comes along and plays across the surface of the ocean and this agitates the ocean's surface so that portions of the ocean rise up into the air and expand into the light. We call these portions of the 'ocean-in-movement' waves."

"What is the takeaway from this?" I asked.

"It seems the ocean can be moved to experience what is above or beyond its condition of being at rest. It does this by expanding its surface, rising upward and rolling forward. Based on this, we develop stories about waves and their paths of seeking, striving, transforming, perfecting, and attaining."

"And by telling stories like this, we come to imagine that there actually IS such a thing as a wave," I added. "But in reality, there is only the ocean."

"Indeed," he continued. "We create paths, goals, measures of success, and all manner of spiritual narratives to complicate the simple fact that all our notions and stories are written on water. They are ephemeral. The ocean's superficial movements have no intrinsic meaning apart from the fact that all waves are always the ocean. And the ocean is indescribable."

"When the ocean rests in a state of abiding," I ventured, "it knows itself directly as its own existence. There is no becoming. There is knowledge by identity. There is fullness and completeness. There is emptiness of any story or notion about waves and their essence or their meanings. There is only the ocean at rest. And this conscious existence is Wisdom."

"You have it!" he asserted, with a broad smile. "Anything beyond that is sheer invention, not Wisdom. Wisdom reveals itself in silence. Silence is peace, which is the feeling-tone of existence."

"Existence," I added, "is conscious."

"Indeed," he confirmed. "And consciousness is always arising in waves of experience in multifarious forms designated as "this" and "that". But when the arising waves subside, consciousness knows itself to be the bliss of existence. This is a mystery unutterable, inconceivable, complete."

"Therefore, we have existence, consciousness and bliss. We have the ocean abiding, arising, and subsiding into its own depth where it rests in awareness of its inherent completeness, its innate bliss. Whether we call this "Wisdom", or "Love", or "God", or "Cosmos", it is what it is, beyond any of our concepts or stories about its form or its essence, or its meaning, and so on."

"You have it!" he confirmed.

I experienced the odd sensation of having channeled Lama Atal to himself.

At this point, he did something surprising. He stepped forward and gave me a big hug. Then, he held me at arm's length and smiled. He then turned and left.

I stood there for a while, in silence. There was no wish for any intervention of mental chatter.

I sat to meditate on the bench where Lama would normally sit.

For a long, long time, I sat there in stillness, immersed in the oceanic depth, feeling whole and fulfilled in a state of utter stillness and peace. I had come home. Homecoming is bliss. The wave-form of my separate self subsided into the ocean of being.

The sun was high in the sky before I stood up and returned to the interior of my tiny hermitage, feeling complete and at peace.

18

The Ocean of Wisdom

Lama Atal's departure was sudden and unannounced. I was missing him for several weeks, meditating alone in the mornings and continuing to review his teachings in my mind when I received a letter informing me that he had taken up residence in Wat Umong, in the city of Chiangmai, located in Northern Thailand. He extended me an invitation to visit him in this beautiful, forested monastery, which had caves constructed many centuries previously for the use of its resident contemplatives.

In his letter, Lama Atal referred to an ancient text called the "Astavakra" which he wanted me to study. He explained that it was "the next step" in my opening up to non-dual Wisdom. He included a hand-written sequence of passages from this work for special consideration:

**Waves, foam, and bubbles do not differ from water.
In the same way, all this which has emanated from
oneself is no other than oneself.**

**All this appears in me, imagined due to ignorance,
just as a snake appears in the rope, the mirage of water
in the sunlight, and silver in mother of pearl.**

**Truly it is in the infinite ocean of myself that, stimulated
by the colourful waves of the world, everything suddenly
arises in the wind of consciousness.**

**In the infinite ocean of myself, the wind of thought
subsides, and the world boat of the living-being traders is
wrecked by lack of goods.**

**How wonderful it is that in the infinite ocean of myself
the waves of living beings arise, collide, play, and disappear,
in accordance with their nature.**

Who can be compared to the great-souled person whose

mind is free from desire even in disappointment, and who has found satisfaction in self-knowledge?

All this arises out of you, like a bubble out of the sea. Knowing yourself like this to be but one, you can find peace.

I am like the ocean, and the multiplicity of objects is comparable to a wave. To know this is knowledge, and then there is neither renunciation, acceptance nor cessation of it.

In the infinite ocean of myself the world boat drifts here and there, moved by its own inner wind. I am not put out by that.

Whether the world wave of its own nature rises or disappears in the infinite ocean of myself, I neither gain nor lose anything by that.

It is in the infinite ocean of myself that the mind-creation called the world takes place. I am supremely peaceful and formless, and I remain as such.

Let the world wave rise or subside according to its own nature in you, the great ocean. It is no gain or loss to you.

It is through your ignorance that all this exists. In reality you alone exist. Apart from you there is no one within or beyond samsara.

Knowing that all this is just an illusion, one becomes free of desire, pure receptivity, and at peace, as if nothing existed.

Only one thing has existed, exists and will exist in the ocean of being. You have no bondage or liberation. Live happily and fulfilled.

Being pure consciousness, do not disturb your mind with thoughts of "for" and "against". Be at peace and remain happily in yourself, the essence of joy.

In him for whom the ocean of samsara has dried up, there is neither attachment or aversion. His gaze is vacant, his behaviour purposeless, and his senses inactive.

I read the text over and over. At times, certain passages would have the effect of drawing my mind into a state of silence and peace. After a few days, I wrote back to Lama Atal informing him of my decision to relocate from Hua Hin to Chiangmai in order to resume our spiritual exchanges.

This proved quite easy to do. I took a bus from Wat Kao Takiap to the station in Hua Hin, and caught a train to Bangkok with connections to

Chiangmai. Within two days of my decision to relocate, I was sitting with Lama Atal on his verandah on a treed hillside overlooking a large water reservoir surrounded by trees, pathways and pavilions in the heart of Wat Umong, Chiangmai. It was a forest with contemplative hermits on the edge of the city.

Between sips of green tea, we discussed the recent past, and I learned that a German monk named Phra Santitthito (Santi), a long-standing friend of Lama Atal's, had been asked to give a series of talks at various meditation centers in Europe, which meant that his "kuti" or cottage had become available.

Most afternoons, friends of Prah Santi would come by expecting to see him. In that way, Lama Atal, as his stand-in, had made the acquaintance of quite a few English and German-speaking spiritual seekers.

With his help, I was able to rent a house within a walled compound not far away on Soi Wat Umong, and by means of a rented motorcycle, it was possible to visit my spiritual teacher most afternoons. In the weeks that followed, the numbers of visitors slowly thinned out until finally we had unbroken free time to talk and meditate.

One afternoon, at the height of the dry season, when the water in the pond was low and the leaves of the trees seemed to be wilting in the extreme heat, I turned to a passage from the Astavakra Samhita which Lama Atal had sent me. As I looked over the verses, penned in his hand, the meditative mood in which I had studied the text several months earlier came back.

Lama Atal opened his copy of the complete text and turned to the page on which the stanzas were printed. He then began to read them, one by one, in a slow and deliberate voice. When he came to one particular verse, he read it twice, and then paused to meditate:

It is in the infinite ocean of myself that the mind-creation called the world takes place. I am supremely peaceful and formless, and I remain as such.

After a long meditative silence, he spoke: "What is real is always being what it is, just as the sun is always shining, even if clouds of daydreaming and thinking obscure the sun, from the perspective of an earthling. The light of nirvana is eternally uncorrupted by obscured perspectives of all kinds. A mirror is still perfectly reflective, even when dust settles on its surface. The power of this truth is so compelling that we have simply to let go, relax and do nothing to experience directly that: "this is how it is".

"The ocean condenses into ice blocks here and there," I replied. "They float about and knock into each other, and they make noises and exchange thoughts about having experiences of various kinds. Awareness is operating through all of this, and AS all of this."

"You are awareness," Atal replied. "Tat Twam Asi!"

He paused for a few moments and then continued: "Awareness holds nothing and has nothing to let go of. Awareness is always relaxed. Indeed, awareness has never grasped an experience of awareness."

"And so, when they teach meditators to practice "awareness of awareness", what could it possibly mean?" I queried.

"Meditators try to concentrate on the ineffable," Atal replied, "thinking that this is the practice. But no, it is not the practice."

Because the lama paused, I queried him further. "What then is the practice indicated in these verses?"

"It comes down to a choice between two aspects of Reality, its beingness and its knowingness. You can feel the beingness by simply relaxing into peace and silence. But you cannot see the knowingness by looking for something called "awareness". That is where the confusion comes in."

"I see," I replied. "Relax into silence and you will BE awareness. But try to grasp awareness experientially and you will find nothing. Indeed, you ARE that awareness, so there is no need to seek, contrive or grasp."

"And that is why the counsel to simply BE, like the ocean, in utter silence, is a more useful form of practice, or 'non-practice', isn't it?" Lama Atal stated the conclusion succinctly. "As contrasted with "awareness of awareness", for example," he added.

"This is very helpful!" I replied.

"It took me years to arrive at this understanding." Lama Atal replied.

"I know I'm repeating myself," I exclaimed, "but some of the teachings can be impossibly misleading! All this talk about practising awareness of awareness can be confusing. The idea that awareness could be grasped by paying attention to it is not true. Fixating on the ocean as if it were some kind of "this" or "that".... well, it's just more selfing-activity."

"Thoughts and labels about imaginary multiple parts," Atal replied, "all of it. Waves are not "parts" of the ocean. They are the ocean manifesting its potential in form, in movement. Ice blocks knock about and make noise, as you say. Such noises are something inconsequential. Noise cannot grasp Wisdom."

He looked at the manuscript again, and said:

"This, however, is not inconsequential:

Only one thing has existed, exists and will exist

In the ocean of being.

You have no bondage or liberation.

Live happily and fulfilled."

Lama Atal's voice trailed off as he finished reading these words from the Astavakra Gita. We both slipped back into meditation.

On the grounds of Wat Umong.

The forest temple known as Wat Umong was a wonderful place to walk, a peaceful, shaded reserve of 15 acres on the edge of Chiangmai, nestled close to the mountain known as Doi Suthep. There were small, simple huts for contemplative monks at various locations among the trees, and an extensive system of man-made caves dating back to the eleventh or twelfth century AD.

This forest temple had a fine library where I would go to do research on Buddhism. This is where I came across a classic book on the Jhanas, the Visuddhimagga, considered the most important Theravada text outside of the Tipitaka canon of scriptures.

Here at Wat Umong, I made friends with Prah Santititto, a German monk who gave generously of his time and advice for those interested in spiritual matters. And it was here that I was able to reconnect with Lama Atal, and deepen the process of spiritual awakening which had begun at my hermitage overlooking the Gulf of Siam.

19

The Cave

It is a strange fact that, although everyone wants to be happy, and happiness has so much to do with being where your heart feels at home, the world is full of people having all kinds of adventures that complicate their lives. This is a universal condition, of course, but I never saw so much of it as when I lived in Southeast Asia. The influence of Hinduism and Buddhism is still very strong in India, Burma, Nepal, Thailand and Laos. Religion and spirituality are widely respected in this part of the world. However, surviving, getting rich, making babies and having fun still preoccupy most of the folks for most of their time.

One of the surprising features of monks in Thailand is that many or most of them pass a very relaxed life in the urban temples where they live. There are a number of forest monasteries where meditation is taken seriously, of course, and Wat Umong is one of those. But in the cities, the life of a monk has much to do with going out for food in the morning, smoking and chatting through much of the day, chanting in the afternoon, and generally enjoying life the rest of the time in any way that distracts from boredom.

Many of the monks are in robes temporarily to make merit for their parents, which means that their monastic experience is thought of as temporary rather than a lifelong vocation. They all seem to have great respect for Buddhism, and they do generally try not to break their vows or disregard their two hundred-plus rules too conspicuously or egregiously. But the lax atmosphere of the urban temples does not encourage a serious application to meditation or study. There are wise, sincere and scholarly monks here and there, as well as a few who are psychics and healers. But for most, life is pleasantly relaxed.

I opened a meditation center in Chiangmai in 1990 and taught university at CMU during the five years of my stay in Northern Thailand. When I first visited the hamlet of Tandokmai, which is about seventy kilometers from my home in Chiangmai, and wandered through the surrounding hills and orchards, I was struck by the natural beauty of the countryside. A friend offered me land in a longan orchard. I built a country home there, intending to use it as a rural retreat from the hectic city life in Chiangmai. After spending some time there, I quickly became aware of how rich in local lore the place really was.

About one half mile from my home among the trees near Tandokmai, I discovered an abandoned temple. The local people told me that it was about one hundred years old. The grounds were quite overgrown with grasses and weeds.

Not far from the temple, a large hill was being quarried for limestone which was the basis of a local cement and construction industry. Many of the very young and elderly people in Tandokmai spent their days with little hammers breaking up limestone rocks into gravel for ridiculously low pay. However, the most interesting feature in the landscape was a cave situated about five minutes' walk from my front door, near the top of a hill which overlooked the entire valley.

It had been used time out of mind by itinerant monks as a shelter from rain and the heat of the sun, and as a place to meditate.

The cave had a wooden floor and a small altar made of cement. From the mouth of this cave, you could see the treetops of mango, lychee and longan orchards and extensive rice fields in the valley below. Oftentimes, a smoky haze would settle over the valley as a result of burning the husks of the recent rice crop. In the dry season, vegetation on the hill would wilt and turn brown, and grass fires would occasionally sweep over the hill leaving large, blackened areas of ash, and scorching the lower branches of the stunted trees.

This hill and others nearby had once been lushly forested, but most of the trees were cut down for quick profit in the 1960's and 70's. As a result of deforestation, water shortages had become endemic and now the stream which ran through the valley at the base of the hill was dry for several months of the year. When riding my motorcycle from Chiangmai to my rural retreat, I could see large desert-like areas, the result of this foolish and unscrupulous destruction of the trees on the hills. When the trees are cut, the soil on the hills can no longer hold rainwater and it gets washed down into the valleys. In Northern Thailand, the rain comes only for two or three months and the rest of the year is very dry. Now, even the great Mae Ping River which was once an artery of commerce and a route for boating into the interior is only a few feet deep and largely silted up. The balance of nature has been seriously disturbed with the result that the weather is often dry, dusty and unbearably hot.

Within the cave was a rock ledge, and on this ledge, too high to be reached, were a number of large wooden boxes. I once clambered up to look inside the boxes, and discovered that they were filled with Buddhist scriptures written in the traditional style on palm leaves. The writing was done by scratching the leaf surface with a sharp stylus and then rubbing charcoal dust over the surface. When the extra powder was brushed away, the incised letters would hold enough of the black dust to be readable. This kind of writing was the traditional way of recording and preserving the Theravada Buddhist scriptures for millennia. A scrap of this ancient writing was lying loose, outside its box, and so I took it back to Chiangmai to have it assessed at the university.

The professional opinion of the qualified university professor was that this was a Buddhist sutra written in the old Lanna (Northern Thai) script. Several people at the university expressed interest in visiting and examining this trove of ancient sutra manuscripts. I felt that they should be photographed so that if they were ever lost or stolen there would be some permanent record, perhaps on microfilm, in some safe library.

It seems that the authorities in Bangkok had instituted a program of travelling around to places such as this cave and gathering up the local artifacts for storage. It was thus quite unusual to find a trove of old sutras which had not been carted off to the capital city. Much of the heritage of the North had been removed to the south of Thailand, leaving it culturally and archaeologically quite denuded.

Apparently, the local monks and villagers knew about this treasure-trove of ancient scriptures, and they were happy and proud that it was still there. They would certainly have objected to anyone disturbing it, but in the early 1990's, no one had done so. My efforts to interest the university in recording these documents came to nothing. And although I felt that the sutras were not secure in that location, there was nothing more I could do. For all I know, they may still be there waiting for some expert in that field of study to determine their contents and scholarly importance. The conditions in the cave are not very secure, because bats roost in and around the boxes, leaving their droppings and their pungent smells. In all probability, mice and other rodents make their homes in among the boxes too. It is remarkable that a national treasure like this was so under-appreciated.

An ever stranger story came to my attention concerning a cave which was located further up the hill, above the one I just described. This cave has a small entrance which was walled up many years ago by the local people. During World War II, the Japanese had gone around gathering up all the valuables they could lay their hands on, especially gold and precious stones. The villagers had collected their valuables and stored them in this upper cave, walling up the entrance for protection. Then, after the war, they reclaimed their belongings and the cave entrance was again sealed. Why seal a cave in which nothing of value was being kept?

It seems that just prior to World War II, a local man had done some searching in the cave, and had discovered a ceremonial boat made of solid gold, an artifact of considerable value. He sold it and pocketed the money, but in the eyes of the villagers he became the object of contempt and hostility. In Thailand, especially among old people in the remote villages, there are quite a few superstitions and taboos about this sort of thing. At the time that I was using the lower cave with the sutras for meditation, this individual was still alive, but very old.

He was poor and alone, living out his final days in a temple in Chiangmai, convinced that he had incurred some very serious karma for stealing and then selling this relic.

While I spent time at my rural retreat near Tandokmai, from time to time travelling monks would come to engage in periods of extended meditation. This kind of monk, from the forest tradition, would walk from one end of the country to the other, living on voluntary food offerings and using much of the free time for study and mediation.

One of these in particular, I remember, carried a big book with him, a book about meditation and the spiritual life written in Thai. He was a monk who never lay down to sleep. He would only doze off occasionally in the sitting posture. Monks like this are the exception, not the rule, in modern Thailand.

Generally, there is less respect for monks now than in previous times, and the lifestyle of the urban monks does little to restore their former veneration. Monks are no longer at the heart of Thai society, as they once were when temples were centers of education, healing, the performing arts, counselling and religion. I quickly came to realize how rare and precious it was to have crossed paths with a real master like Lama Atal.

On a hill quite close to the one I have been describing, there was another old temple. It became quite popular in the 1970's because one of the monks who lived there had all kinds of remarkable abilities. One day, the story goes, while the king of Thailand was flying from Bangkok to Chiangmai, he looked out the window of his plane and was surprised to see this particular monk flying through the air!

The king later visited and talked to the monk and would consult him from time to time on various questions. Royal notice helped to bring public attention to this miracle-working monk, and word quickly spread concerning his other special abilities such as seeing the future, bi-locating and reading peoples' minds. These were talents he had developed through the practice of meditation. As a result of all this attention, quite a few monks came to live and practice meditation at this temple, and quite a few cells were constructed for them to inhabit. But after the miracle-working monk died, interest quickly faded and the monastery fell into decay.

When I visited the site, the cells (or "kutis' as they are called in Thai) were virtually all empty. The place was practically deserted, with only a handful of monks still living there, sleeping off the heat of the afternoon, and a few thin dogs wandering around. The temple was lonely and neglected, hot and windy. It had a desolate feeling. I suspected that it would never again see its former glory.

Although monks are forbidden to display occult abilities in public, the Thai people are always eager to know about monks who have these unusual talents. Fortune telling is quite common among monks.

On one occasion, I was taken by a friend and his wife to a Burmese monk in Chiangmai who would reveal people's future fortunes. There were a number of people waiting for a consultation because he was very accurate in predicting the future and telling people how to get past their problems.

This monk told me that I had excellent karma from past lives, very few problems in this life, and that he would write me a letter of introduction to the Patriarch (leading monk) of Burma, whom he encouraged me to meet. I was told that serious meditation and the most advanced meditators are not to be found in Thailand, but rather in Burma where modernization had not yet corrupted the people and where one can still experience the old intensity and devotion to spirituality. It did not feel like the right time to visit Burma, and I was not particularly interested in Theravada Buddhism, but I kept an open mind to the possibility of taking up this invitation at some future time.

From the mouth of my cave, you could see the villagers in their straw hats planting, tending and harvesting their rice and walking to and fro from the village. You could see white cattle in some of the fields, long-horns looking like those of India. But you could also hear the constant rumble of traffic on the road, and you could feel that life was quickly changing. It was clear that the past was receding into history and a very different life was dawning all across Northern Thailand. For hundreds, perhaps thousands of years, this cave had looked out over the valley and seen myriads of people come and go. It had given some of them shelter, and protected their sacred scriptures. It had outlived empires and seen the rise and fall of forests, temples, village and cities. What would the future hold? And how long could the religious traditions of Thailand endure the face of these changing influences?

What I learned from spending time in this cave is that one can truly come home to the inner peace and fullness only by letting go of all the distracting needs and interests that keep the egoic mind and body busy going here and there and doing this and that. For me, the cave was a place which offered an invitation to go deep within and discover what was ultimately real. But I knew also that the real sanctuary is the cave of the heart, and the real treasure of the real cave can never be ancient scriptures written on palm leaves.

Having spent time on a busy international university campus in the heart of a vibrant city, having meditated in a beautiful hermitage overlooking the Gulf of Siam, and now having spent time in a cave overlooking a rural valley, I came to understand that the real refuge can never be a particular location in 3D time and space. Even a legendary cave with a hidden treasure of ancient scriptures could not substitute for the refuge within. For I had discovered and experienced the domain where the thinking mind melts into the heart of loving wisdom and returns to the truth of its existence. This meant that the wave-form of the separate self was ready to subside and merge in the blissful ocean.

Antique Thai silk is perfect material for hot-weather clothing. I was fortunate to own a few shirts made from antique silk, which was becoming hard to find.

In this photo, I am wearing antique Thai silk, the many virtues of which I came to appreciate. Foremost of these was the fact that this material is the coolest kind of fabric that a person can wear in a country where the temperatures generally range between thirty and forty degrees Celsius. There was a tailor at the end of the Soi (street) who would make up shirts for me in various styles, using sarongs of antique Thai silk which I could purchase in the downtown market place in the walled city of Chiangmai.

These antique silks were colored with natural dyes, and had been hand-woven in the villages of Northern Thailand in the first half of the twentieth century. They were already becoming hard to find in these villages because buyers had discovered that visitors to Thailand loved to acquire them.

The tropical climate had its benefits. On my left is a banana plant, and on my right a papaya. Eating home-grown fresh fruit was one of the joys of living in this tropical country!

I was quite surprised when, one day, a group of locals descended on the large fruit tree located outside my front door to harvest virtually all the fruit, with the explanation that the owner of the property had given them the right to do so. Since he had generously allowed me to build a home on his property, I took this abrupt harvest graciously. "Go with the flow, live and learn" became my motto.

20

The Ocean At Rest

On my last visit to Lama Atal, at his "kuti" in Wat Umong, he presented me with a gift, a hand-written manuscript, wrapped in crimson silk like a traditional Tibetan book. Along with this gift, he offered me a succinct but meaningful comment:

"Make this your foundational study," he said. "Come back to it again and again. Live, breathe and assimilate the wisdom in these lines. They are the essence of supreme realization. If you find my comments on this text incomplete or wanting, by all means add your own insights. This document pulls together everything we have talked about, and everything we have contemplated. Keep the spirit of our time together alive by making this wisdom your very own."

I learned with regret that Lama Atal would be leaving the next day. When would we cross paths again in this lifetime? I felt a pang of loss.

In Thailand, I studied this text repeatedly. When I returned to Canada, it was packed up with my journals and notes and did not see the light of day for almost thirty years. Now, I treasure it beyond all measure. In this spirit, I offer it to you.

The Ocean At Rest

By Longchenpa, and Commentary by Lama Atal

Neither emanating or gathering,
Awakened state of self-clarity,
This is the equal state of a clear and
Motionless ocean;
Dharmata clear to the depths,
Self-rising state of wisdom;
Resting free from arising, entering, hope, and fear.

The ocean at rest is clear and awake, not actively doing anything. It exists in a state of motionless quiescence. There is no hope, no fear, no taking in or putting out, no going anywhere. The ocean is thus in a state of *being* rather than *doing*. This is how reality presents itself when the egoic thinking activity of the mind subsides. There is a sense of profound depth and utter clarity.

The ocean is clear knowingness which has no need to do anything or to go anywhere, a state of completeness and completion, inherently whole and at peace.

In an ocean unrippled by wind,
Planets and stars arise.

The appearance of planets and stars
Is not something beyond the water
And does not hide it.

Just so, objects ceaselessly appear
In the transparent, awakened state.

Undefiled by fixation, they rest
Without moving from rigpa
And the awakened state.

There are times when the surface of the ocean is agitated by wind. Within human consciousness, thinking activity is driven by such winds. Emotional reactivity is also wind-driven. These winds bring motion to the otherwise tranquil and peaceful resting state of the ocean. In stillness, the un-agitated, mirror-like quality of the ocean's knowingness can reflect the forms and the radiance of various lights, mere appearances that are not other than mind itself, nor elsewhere. Every wave is only an appearance of the ocean.

Reflections on the surface of the water do not alter the nature of the water. In the same way, forms appear to knowingness, but do not alter the pristine nature of this very knowingness that apprehends them. In our daily lived experience, forms appear ceaselessly within the transparency of consciousness.

This awakeness is inherent to mind, not something that needs to be generated or sustained. In Yoga, this awakeness is the goal. It is also the path. This means that striving and attaining are pointless. Although mere appearances arise within the space of the mind, if they are not "grasped" and fixated upon, they do not obscure the pristine clarity of self-recognizing wisdom. When attention is preoccupied with conceptually designated fixations, however, the self-recognizing insight of rigpa is clouded. Rigpa exists, but the grasping mind has fixated its power of attention elsewhere. Non-distraction sustains recognition of rigpa's presence. Of course, rigpa is present whether we recognize it or not. But wisdom consists in knowing and continuously seeing thoughts for what they are (rather than pursuing them).

Ignorance hungers for experience, grasping and fixating on thoughts.

> **In the pure realization of the chokshak**
> **(let-be as-is)**
> **Of an ocean,**
> **There is no appearance, nor any maker of it.**
>
> **It is not empty; emptiness does not exist.**
> **It is not luminous,**
> **But is the sphere of the**
> **great luminosity.**
>
> **It is not drowsy, and it has no discursiveness.**
> **It has not gone beyond itself, and never will.**

It was and is not disturbed,
Transcending all disturbance.
It does not arise
By having been produced.

Realization of the nature of the ocean depends on letting-be, or "letting go". This is the only way to experience reality as it is. Beingness (Sanskrit: *sat*) does not present itself as a particular form or appearance. Nor is it a "doer". It cannot be grasped by conceptual designations such as "empty". Reality does not exist in the same way that conceptual designations are imagined to exist as being "this" rather than "that".

Although radiance and light are attributes of the ultimate reality, the Absolute is unqualified in any way.

It does not lose awareness to obscurity. It never becomes other than it is. It is not agitated, and is not the product of anything that preceded it. Unqualified beingness, discovered by letting go, is alone real.

Take a look at this,
which is the great means of resting.
Not performing any emanating or gathering,
This is the single state of resting known as chokshak (let-be as-is).

It is not existent,
but not beyond (seeming) existence.

You do not have to perform tantric practices of emanating or gathering to look into and experience this ultimate reality. You have only to become still. This is done by letting go of thoughts. Relax. Allow what is to simply be. Do not try to verbalize or label it as "this" or "that", existent or non-existent. Just relax, let be, and become the experience of the ocean as it is.

In the secret wisdom which is like an ocean,
Rest in self-existent, universal space;

Here disturbance has never ever come to pass.
That is the way it has been from all eternity.

When you come to rest in what is ultimately real, and know it as it is in its utter spaciousness, you will have arrived at the deepest and most secret wisdom. There can be no agitation in this ultimacy. It is the space in which all things have arisen.

It is self-existent, beyond time
and beyond appearances.

From the great ocean whose depth
is difficult to measure,
The victory banner that does not
diminish is viewed as the peak.

Without emptying mind,
the kaya of the great uncreated,
the unproduced is victorious
over all production.

The ocean of infinite consciousness is experienced as being immeasurably deep and impossible to reckon. From the point of view of a human mind, homecoming to this ultimate reality is considered a victory, the supreme victory. But for whom? It is by letting go of the contents of the mind that the Absolute is recognized. This is not a victory which can be created or produced. It is beyond all of the forms or movements that arise within its spaciousness.

This is the uncreated resting known as chokshak.
(letting-be as-is)

Eternally it has never risen into existence.
Appearance is not transformed;
Mind is not created.

This is what is realized by resting in Dharmata.

We circle back again and again to the recognition that simply letting go and abiding in pure and simple Being is the Way. Be clear on this point: the uncreated can never be generated by any form of activity. Transforming appearances is not the Way. The effort to generate what cannot be generated is similarly mistaken. Simply let go of all that is impermanent and rest in the realization of what remains. THAT alone is real.

Since the wisdom of the state of Dharmakaya
Has completely abandoned any kind of thoughts,

If there is no production of discursive flickering,
By that the intention of meditation is fulfilled.

To rest in what is ultimately real is to abide in Wisdom. In this state of pure being, all thoughts and thinking activity are absent. That condition of awareness where all tendency toward thinking has dissolved is the true end of meditation. Come home. Rest in that state.

If partial conceptions of objects
have not been fixated,
They rise like planets and stars within
the depths of the ocean.
Un-fixated luminosity is unobstructed.

The way of being of realization is like that.

For the awakened mind, appearances still arise. But if you do not grasp at them conceptually, the clear light of awareness will be unobscured and the state of realization continues on, uncompromised. The ocean reflects the forms which light continues to manifest, but letting go of thoughts and thinking activity allows awareness to reveal its pristine luminosity.

Deluded ones, unskilled in tantra,
just say whatever comes out.

Some of them, attached to texts
Which they only partially understand, think:
"These four chokshaks are the means
of resting of thögal."

This is incorrect teaching
That cannot be put into practice.
The opening lotus without letters
Has been joined to spurious words
And one-sided partiality.
This joins it to all partialities whatsoever.
"The Precious Sign-Throne of Appearance
Is joined to all partialities," as is said.

The tantric scriptures are sometimes conceived to be a means to an end, as if understanding, interpreting and putting them into action leads to realization. People who try to read and interpret these words in this way arrive at incomplete and misdirected notions about reality in terms of its being a goal which can be attained by striving. This is delusion. Taking appearances as the goal can only lead to distorted and partial under-standing. To study and practice in this way is to follow a mistaken view.

> **In Trekchö and Thögal,**
> **What needs to be known**
> **Is the root of everything.**
>
> **This is transparent insight revealed in nakedness.**
> **If one does not know this,**
> **Whatever else one joins to oneself**
> **Will be of no use.**
>
> **The great meditators of Trekchö**
> **Will mix themselves with the path of all delusions.**

In the principal practices of Ati Yoga, recognition of the true nature of the ocean is of the essence. This insight alone, in its purity, is the key to abiding in Wisdom. If the nature of the ocean is not recognized, the various forms of practice, whether active or passive, will only mislead. Even the practice of Trekchod is compromised by delusion when the ocean is not recognized as it truly is.

> **By going through the means of grasping the mind,**
> **They will not transcend samsara.**
>
> **Thögel will stray into the realm of form**
> **By being attached to things and characteristics.**

Efforts to control thinking activity or to fixate on the nature of mind do not lead to nirvana. Even the practice of Thogal goes astray if the goal is not truly recognized and taken as the Way. It is easy to get preoccupied by the ocean's waves and diverted into considerations of forms and qualities.

First and foremost, recognize the pristine and spacious nature of the ocean in itself, as it is, unqualified and pure. Take that as the singular Way, and let be. Make this be your sole method, whether in Trekchod or Thogal.

Therefore, recognizing unobstructed,
naked awareness is very important.

It is not enough just to know this.
One has to master and stabilize it.

Introduction to the nature of mind is indispensable. This is the only way to know the ocean as it is. One insight alone will not do.

It is necessary for the insight to become continuous and to replace preoccupation with the ocean's waves.

Not going beyond that state is very important.
Therefore, among the many means of resting
That have been taught,
One must first prepare one's place
By realizing the chokshak of an ocean.
Then one should diligently practice it.

Cultivate this state of abiding known as 'being as the ocean'. It is free of thinking activity. It is pure beingness, knowing its own existence as it is. This condition of being at rest is first and foremost in importance. It is simply a matter of letting go and being at peace in the pristine, thought-free space that is alone real when all that moves or appears remains un-grasped and un-conceptualized. This can only be practiced if there is prior recognition of the nature of the ocean as it is. Once recognized, the experience of abiding as the ocean is to be cultivated continuously.

Also in regard to the details of cutting off the strayings, the Thaljur says:

As for the meditation of resting without any straying,
The gates of the senses dwell
in a state of luminosity.

Mind does not flicker
With discursive conceptualizations.
The mind that produces analysis within awareness,
As one is not lost in externals,
Is without existence.

The wind of discursive thought will at times stir up waves on the ocean's surface. Interest in varied forms and their motions may arise. But if the ocean is known as it truly is, these externals will be recognized for what they are. They all lack true existence.

They are mere appearances, like a mirage or an echo or the form of a snake in a rope. Take this to be your supreme method for getting free from distraction.

"Fixating luminosity in the style of partiality,"
Means habitually thinking that
External appearances are "this and that."

"Those who transform themselves
By means of colors and letters,"
Are those who fixate inner mind
By conceptual examination.
The rest is easy to understand.

If the reflections in a mirror are known to be mere appearances which cannot truly exist as either "this" or a "that", then you will find freedom from preoccupation with such appearances. The light of awareness need not be involved in analysis of mere appearances.

The consciousness of the ocean need not be distracted by considerations of its endless waves. If you use meditative techniques to concentrate the mind and examine its contents in detail, thinking that you can ultimately transform the mind by such methods, there will be no end of misdirected activity. Be clear on this point and you will have no difficulty with other aspects of the yoga.

If those who transform themselves
By means of colors and letters
Do not fall into partialities of that kind,
That is the meditation of resting without straying.

> If you are free of this compulsion to try and better yourself by meditative self-cultivation that relies on various forms and sounds, you will have no difficulty in remembering and realizing that you are the ocean at rest.

* * * * *

Months later, when he had settled into a new living situation, Lama Atal sent me a letter in which he referred to this text, and repeated his suggestion that I take it as the basis of my study and practice. He wrote: "When, in meditation, you become the ocean at rest, whatever appears to the mind is recognized as mere appearance, not more than reflections on water or a mirage in the desert. The background, the ground of being, does not appear. From time to time, the energies that generate movement and appearance will subside into a state of almost total stillness, and there will be the experience of sinking into a state of profound release from which there is no desire or will to emerge. This is a return to the natural bliss of being, or you may say, the Source. I wish finally to share a few words with you that came to me from entering the ocean directly:

The ocean at rest
Abides in the peace
Of its true condition.

This is called existence.

The ocean at rest
Abides in the knowledge
Of its true condition.

This is called consciousness.

The ocean at rest
Abides in the fullness
Of its true condition.

Which is bliss, eternal and complete.

Lama Atal

Aunt Rose visits me in Chiangmai.

My aunt Rose was 82 years old when she flew out from Toronto to spend a couple of weeks with me in Chiangmai. We traveled everywhere in the city on my motorbike which was both the most convenient and the most economical mode of transportation.

This photo is taken outside the gate of a compound which I rented for ten thousand bhat per month. You can see two papaya plants behind the iron gateway, grown from seed and ready to bear fruit. I had a few small rooms constructed, which you can also see in the background, where serious students of meditation could visit or live.

Early each morning, the students and I had a routine of hatha yoga, meditation and a short talk. Then, we would have breakfast, and after that each person would be free to go his or her way and begin the business of the day.

I came to appreciate the cool morning temperatures because they afforded the best time for yoga and meditation, whereas by the afternoon, the temperature would range from the low thirties into the low forties, Celsius, making any kind of endeavor burdensome.

21

A Way Forward

A few days before I left Thailand to take up residence again in Canada, I received this final letter from Lama Atal:

> Dear Friend,
>
> Although physical distance separates us, I have been feeling some of the upheaval which you are experiencing. Now that we can no longer speak and meditate together, you may be asking: "What is the way forward?" What I wish to share with you in this letter is an answer to this question.
>
> We have shared deep meditations and profound spiritual teachings. But as you know, the essential element in any teaching lies not in the words but rather in the sincerity and dedication of the one who reads and applies them. The attitude and intent that you bring to your practice is as important as the practice itself, or even more so! From all the different forms of practice you have come to know, you need to find a way of applying a single, core practice that is suited to your temperament and character. And this is what I have shared with you. No one can tell you *how* to practice your chosen way. You discover this by trial and error. It has been thus for all the masters throughout history. And the way that you apply a meditation technique is likely to evolve also, as your realization deepens.
>
> The starting point for a human mind is that there IS a wave and that it can supposedly find a way forward. From this perspective, the conventional teaching is as follows: What counts most is the power of your intent to identify with the truth of your being in

this lifetime. This is what will bring you home to your inmost refuge. This is how you will come to know, with complete confidence, that you ARE freedom itself.

Form the clear and firm intention to directly sense the inmost depth of your being. Summon up a heartfelt, living experience of what is most real for you, as you yourself experience and feel it. *Be faithful to your own immediate and direct experience, here and now, beyond notions and wishful thinking.* Your meditation is simply being true to who you feel yourself to be, in the depths of your heart, beyond all notions or recollected teachings.

Simply release everything that is in the head, and drop down into the space of the heart and abide there in stillness. I cannot over-emphasize the importance and value of making this your core practice. This is your way forward. Everything else that I may share with you in this letter is but a footnote to this single, vital point. Be fully confident in the experience that comes to you when you practice in this way.

There is no need to pretend to be any particular personality beyond or in addition to who you really feel that you are in the depth of your heart. You certainly are not this body, or this mind. They exist within the spaciousness of the truth of your being. You are awake, loving and liberated consciousness beyond any and every notion or story.

If you hold the intent to experience each and every moment from your true nature, you will realize that you never really needed or even cared about all the things you imagined to be necessary for happiness.

When you relate to life from your heart, from spiritual openness, you will discover that you ARE the way forward, and your heart is your sure compass. You will not need further studies about how to practice, or how your sitting meditations relate to your life. Your own heart, fully awake to the immediacy of this moment, will reveal your way forward to you in every instant of experience.

If you approach your life and your meditation in this manner, anything at all that you might want to do or experience will appear in your life with the natural and effortless ease of the cosmic flow itself.

Perhaps you have not yet come to this degree of inner freedom. Perhaps you live inside a mind which has adopted the idea: 'I am the body'. Do your thoughts sometimes want to run wild and stir up addictive involvements with something that seems other than the truth of your being? If so, just keep coming back to the inner sanctuary and the Presence you know to be real and true.

Permit me to share something your heart already knows, but which your mind may occasionally forget:

Recognize the pure feeling which is completely free of the vagaries of thinking activity. This pure feeling-state has no boundaries or limits. It is innately, naturally, and unconditionally happy. It is the wellspring of peace, wisdom, love and creativity. Be still. Let go of struggle and effort. Your natural state and its feeling tone will shine through as the answer to all your seeking and striving.

You are already the heart, the eternal Self. And yet if this is not your actual, lived experience, it helps to ask: "Why so?"

Be willing to face and address the fact that your mind is addicted to thinking. Be willing to admit that you are intoxicated, distracted, fascinated and confused by thoughts and stories. The implication of this addiction is that you are mostly living inside a thought-bound fantasy.

Interesting as this may be, such an addiction does not really work in your favour. If you wish to be happy, you will need to remember that your heart is your real home. Joy is your true nature. Fulfilment is always beyond the domain of your thinking activity.

And the way home is so simple: drop the mind into the heart.

Enduring happiness is not found in thoughts or in pursuit of thoughts. That is the routine habit of the mind, always to be thinking, reflecting, conceptualizing and pursuing its numberless fantasies. When you realize that this does not make you truly happy, you will at last be willing to bring the restless mind into the heart. You will want above all else to abide continuously in the sanctuary of peace and bliss, where a very special kind of satisfaction will arise.

When you live in your head, all you can do is catch thoughts after they have arisen and then release them. But after you identify with your heart, you can abide in the feeling tone of pure being, and see the thoughts taking shape and disappearing like evanescent phantasms. You can notice thoughts as they arise from the heart, your center of pure being. And you can let them appear and pass away like clouds in the sky of mind.

You will eventually be able to expose and see and study the root thought, which is the "I am this form" thought. You will be able to see it in operation, and you will be able to recognize how it initiates the whole process of thinking-activity. It is the first thought to arise and it fuels the thinking-activity of the mind.

Once this process has been discerned directly, the days of the tyranny of thinking are numbered.

The thought-free awareness that you experience in calm-abiding meditation is not identical to the natural state you experience in the heart, but it has similarities. If you can rest in the thought-free state for an extended period of time in meditation, the heart, your inner being, will come forward and re-orient your experience. *In time, it will eliminate the compulsive habit of thinking-activity so that it falls away, never to return.*

That is why it is important to meditate regularly and deeply. Your way forward is to abide in the thought-free state, and move toward direct experience of the awakened heart, your inmost being.

When you come home to your heart, you will know the power of deep and enduring peace. Moreover, you will recognize peace as your true home.

This differs from most forms of watching meditation where you simply observe your thoughts in a passive way. The spiritual heart, your inner sanctuary, entertains no thoughts at all. It HAS and it IS only peace, love, bliss and wisdom. But you will find that these are more than enough to be truly happy. You will treasure that pure feeling of being free at last.

Thought-free abidance in the true center of your being is the key. If the mind is perpetually busy, then your openness and availability to awakening is very limited. Remember: the heart, the Inner Being, comes to the fore in silence. The way you "get there" is to rest in thought-free, heart-centered quiescence to the best of your ability. You will experience the pure feeling of having coming home to the truth of your being. And this will be for you a source of boundless confidence in the truth of your experience.

At that point, functional thoughts may arise. They make no difference. They do not affect your happiness, take away from your peace or diminish your love.

The mind may try to mislead you with some kind of substitute for the genuine Presence of your inner being. It will give you a neutral state, an experience which is not inwardly alive and not really satisfying. *You have to go deep inside the spiritual heart, into the silence, to feel the real peace which is identical to your awakened Presence.* If you can relax into the heart's depth and silence, you will go beyond this neutral experience and see clearly that it was only a veil or obscurity on the journey home.

So dive into the silence, no matter how brief your visits may be, even a few seconds, and develop this habit of sinking down into your heart. When a thought comes along, release it, drop into the heart once again, and take in the pure feeling of your deepest core.

Cultivate an undying closeness to your inmost being and allow yourself to FEEL its living PRESENCE.

Remember this pure feeling of living Presence. It is indescribable, ineffable, beyond the grasp of words or thoughts. In time, you will come to realize with full confidence which you can never lose that you are THIS. This is what the great masters have always taught. With practice, you will discover how to abide in this pure feeling that is your essence and how to let go of everything else.

Many masters have taught from the perspective of the Ocean which is beyond any notion of separate waves, let alone a way forward. Their non-dual teaching arises spontaneously from recognition that there is no wave, no dilemma, nowhere to go and nothing to do. Talk of seeking, practice, realization and progress all hinge on the idea that there could possibly be a wave that needed to find a way forward because it needed to realize that it was the ocean. That is a dream, a fantasy. The awakened heart will dispel the dream and all its fantasies, dissolving them in the Wisdom that you ARE what you have sought, and could never be other.

You must have noticed that I have made a considerable effort to emphasize and repeat what is of the essence, from the point of view of the wave. But in these words, you may discover at last that the wave-form of your individual mind has merged and become one with the vastness of the Eternal Ocean. You will then remember that you have always been beyond dilemmas because, in the truth of your being you are eternally free.

Your Friend, Lama Atal

22

Postscript

In a handwritten letter, Lama Atal had urged me to "live, breathe and assimilate" the wisdom which he had passed on in Longchenpa's "The Ocean At Rest". He had stated that this precious teaching is "the essence of supreme realization." His commentary on the words of the great Tibetan master revealed the true depth of their timeless wisdom, more acutely meaningful to me personally because of my experiences living beside the ocean. In a most pointed way, Lama Atal had advised: "Keep the spirit of our time together alive by making this wisdom your very own."

In the years since we parted, I had come to appreciate that while high meditative experiences such as the bliss of Nirvana or the Brahman-Consciousness were encouraging and even illumining, they were not, in and of themselves, evidence of assimilation of the the wisdom which Lama Atal had transmitted both by his words and his living presence.

It became more and more clear over time that meditative experiences, however high, are fleeting, and therefore they are not what is being sought. On the other hand, the wisdom and the insights accumulated in the journey of life itself are always present in the cave of the deep heart - even when we may temporarily have forgotten its location. That is where the real treasure is to be found.

I have often been puzzled how, when reading my writings from decades past, the teachings imparted by Lama Atal had been foreshadowed long before I actually met him in person, and this in two ways. In the first instance, I could see how my non-recognition of quintessential insights such as impermanence and emptiness had limited what was possible in terms of spiritual development. And in the second place, I could see that the wisdom of my inner being had always been complete, however unrecognized and unappreciated by me, in my own mind and heart.

Nowhere was this more strikingly clear than in a piece of writing penned some time prior to meeting Lama Atal. Among the aging papers stowed away from decades before, and shipped in a box from Thailand, I found the following:

There Is A Place

There is a place I sometimes go,
In the very core of my existence.
Below the restless thought-waves,
There is a place where I am at peace.
I am not seen by the many,
Nor do I see the many.
I rest in the One.

In deepest rest, empty of agitation,
I feel the fullness of existence,
The fullness that is the ocean.
Grown tired of making waves upon the surface of my life,
I go within to experience the ocean's depth,
Knowing this depth to be the truth of my existence.

Here, in the core of being, I rest alone.
Yet, being alone, I am one with the many.
As love holds the beloved,
Or as the vessel of the heart holds love,
So the ocean of my inmost core
Brings forth the waves that play upon its surface.
And as the ocean brings forth waves,
So the core of my existence claims this vast universe
As a play upon its surface.

In that core, there is completion,
And in that core, I am complete.

The waves rise, and the waves fall.

The waves push and the waves pull.
And those who play among the waves
Rise and fall amid the changing pulls and pushes,
Sometimes happy, sometimes sad.
But in the struggle and the agitation,
The wave-lovers feel they are alive,
And they would not trade this wild wave-dream
within their minds
For any deeper rest.
They fear death.

I do not fear death.
I fear agitation.
I am tired of the restless dreams my mind has played
Upon the surface of my life.

Among the waves of the moving mind,
The tiny form of my separate existence has been waiting,
Waiting for the call that comes from
the core of existence,
Waiting for the remembrance and the realization
Of what always has been known
In the depth of the ocean of being.

Then, finally, it becomes clear:
This moving wave of the agitated mind
has become the ocean,
Entering into all forms or none,
Making forms and moving in them,
Moving through them, and moving beyond them,
But always resting in the beyond,
Beyond them all,
The ocean remembers the waves
Into a place beyond difference.

I am water and ice,

But yet beyond the play of their alternation.
I am the waves that roll shoreward beneath the sky,
Stillness that moves not, and yet moves,
A cosmic flow that is music heard, and unheard.

In rest, and in movement,
Unfolding beyond the world of form,
In the ocean of existence,
Beyond the alternation of the waves,
Into the fullness of the emptiness,
I am being carried.

A Meditation Center in Chiangmai

As predicted while I was living in my hermitage overlooking the ocean, it took time to establish a meditation center in Chiangmai, but it did come into being over a period of several years. We had a collective morning meditation daily, and workshops from time to time, to which the general public was invited. These are photos of one such workshop. The Buddhist worldview was well established in Chiangmai and region, so impermanence, calm abiding, samsara and karma were topics with which people were mostly familiar, and a good place to start.

Upon returning to Canada, I purchased a beautiful and spacious Victorian estate in Lindsay, Ontario as a new meditation center. As you can imagine, the circumstances of a small town in rural Canada are very different from those of Thailand, and especially the oceanside hermitage where I spent so many happy hours. Currently, we meditate on Monday and Thursday evenings, with a daily meditation in the morning, from 9 to 10 am. Feel free to contact me at: calverleyr@yahoo.ca. Any and all questions are welcome.